My Final R

A young sailor's misfortune
on the flight deck of the
USS Forrestal
CV-59

Authors: John Pugioti USN (Ret.) MS Ed.,

Wesley E. Etheridge Sr., USN (Ret.) MTS/DCAMF

outskirtspress
DENVER, COLORADO

Outskirts Press, Inc.
http://www.outskirtspress.com

Paperback ISBN: 978-1-4787-6204-1
Hardback ISBN: 978-1-4787-7533-1

Outskirts Press and the "OP" logo are trademarks belonging to Outskirts Press, Inc.

PRINTED IN THE UNITED STATES OF AMERICA

Special Acknowledgments

Thanks to Verna Hall-Banks, VWK Auto Sales LLC, and GCS Facilitators and Consultants, the "Leading Authority on Military Veterans and Anger Management" for fostering a dynamic that led to an opportunity to write this book. This story primarily came to fruition because of the sacrifices and contributions of each of them, which ensured that Camp Verna, a "trauma-informed care" services and transitional facility for homeless female veterans and others, was available to provide a variety of services, such as PTSD and MST support, anger management, conflict resolution, workforce development, and substance abuse training for military veterans and other individuals in need.

A special acknowledgment also is for John's immediate family—which includes his mother, Mrs. Rosile Pugioti; oldest sister, Elaine; and middle sister, Karen—and for one of his best friends, New York City firefighter Mr. Tommy F. Boland, who is directly responsible for reuniting John and me after almost forty years.

Table of Contents

Acknowledgments

We hereby acknowledge the following people and organizations for their contributions to this book: the men who were there and survived while working on the flight deck of the USS *Forrestal CV-59* on the evening of January 15, 1978; without their eyewitness statements, the unfiltered truth (not the subjective, opaque, never independently verified US Navy version of what happened that evening) would never have come to light, and what they individually encountered that unforgettable and tragic evening would not have been shared via this platform for the entire world to read. Thank you, Jessie Lopez, Jeffery A. West, and Paul L. Cobble.

In addition, we would like to acknowledge and appreciate the sacrifices made by all military servicemen and women in all branches of service, regardless of era, but especially the officers and enlisted individuals who proudly served onboard the USS *Forrestal CV-59*, a United States of America ship that was built at Newport News Shipbuilding Co., Newport News, Virginia, and commissioned on October 1, 1955. At the time of its commissioning, it was the world's first super aircraft carrier, and it became the oldest of its class of aircraft carriers until its decommissioning on September 11, 1993. In early 2014, All Star Metals, a subsidiary of Scrap Metal Services (SMS), proudly announced that it had been awarded a US Navy contract to dismantle and recycle the inactive aircraft carrier on February 14, 2014, in Brownsville, Texas.

This book is also a salute to the long history of service of one of our nation's strongest military assets and treasures—**USS *Forrestal* CV-59**: **fair winds and following seas to the "FID"** for a job well done.

Preface

Courtesy of the "Leading Authority on Military Veterans and Anger Management"

As human beings, we all are fallible; in fact, some of our greatest leaders have achieved victory, prestige, and status because of acknowledging and learning from theirs and others' mistakes. In the World's Greatest Navy, we were taught to believe and live and die by this saying: "safety is always written in someone else's blood," basically meaning that we learn and adopt best practices at the cost of other mistakes.

Again, to be human is to make mistakes, but somehow when men get into positions of authority (especially when they put on the uniform) in organizations of great power and have access to unlimited resources, human capital, other people's money and are endorsed by a systemic culture which validates them based upon their positional authority for protecting our life, liberty, and freedom, the pressure to be perfect in order to project strength in leadership and gain promotions can supersede reality at the cost of resources, human capital, and money.

A hypothetical example could be a very-high-ranking military officer who is the supervisor of a female junior officer. He observes his immediate superior getting intoxicated at a welcome-home-from-deployment celebration, and that supervisor inappropriately gropes the stated junior military female officer, and he eventually coerces her (taking advantage of his positional authority) into capitulating to his advances. Then later, when she is alone and begins to feel guilty and ashamed about what transpired and decides to initiate a written grievance regarding the incident and asks for assistance from her supervisor, not only does he deny observing what happened but he initiates an unfavorable Fit- Rep (officer evaluation) based upon her supposed lack of leadership and a pattern of unfavorable job performance, and in essence he forces her out of the military. In reality, this could have been a scenario in the real-life incident that happened at the infamous 35th Annual Tail Hook Association Symposium, in Las Vegas, Nevada, in September 1991. https://en.wikipedia.org/wiki/Tailhook_scandal

In 2004, Patrick Daniel Tillman, an NFL Player at the time, became a former NFL football player when he left his profession to become a US Army Ranger. On April 22, 2004, it was reported that he was killed in action by enemy fire during a firefight in the mountains of Afghanistan. Controversy ensued, and later it was determined that Pat Tillman was killed as a result of friendly fire. The family and other critics allege that the Department of Defense delayed disclosure for weeks after his memorial service, basically to protect the image of the US Armed Forces. I am sure they were disappointed with the Army's handling of the situation; however, they did get answers that led to the discovery of the truth about what really happened regarding the tragic loss of their beloved Patrick Daniel Tillman, giving them in part some measure of closure about his friendly-fire tragedy. https://en.wikipedia.org/wiki/Pat_Tillman

Again, we are all fallible, but when high levels of leadership, military or otherwise, are allowed to police themselves, it's a systemic problem. Observe all around you in the age of the twenty-four-hour news cycle and just notice that when things go wrong at the highest of levels and it is exposed, transparency is jettisoned to the wayside, and on too many occasions the public, loved ones, and victims get skewed versions of the truth. For an example of how it was done right, I have included a short overview of the most infamous of all flight deck fires.

On July 29–30, 1967, off the coast of Vietnam in the Tonkin Gulf, tragedy struck the USS *Forrestal CV-59* when a Zumi 5" rocket accidently fired into another aircraft, on its flight deck, and almost immediately fuel tank ruptures and multiple explosions simultaneously occurred as a full conflagration engulfed the aft end of the flight deck and rapidly spread to portions of the 03 level of the FID. Brave men courageously fought the intense fires, helped jettison unexpended ordinance and even hot live explosives, while at the same time saving the lives of their fellow shipmates. When it was all over, 134 officers and men had died in the catastrophe, and 161 suffered injuries. It was the worst United States carrier fire since WWII, and it cost to the US Navy $72 million dollars.

There have been extensive stories about the tragedy over the decades that have passed. There is authentic US Navy archive footage, filmed from the plat lens area on the 05 five level, which exhibit full transparency regarding what was happening before, during, and after the catastrophe, and therefore, we have a comprehensive understanding of what initiated the chain of events that day, which led to this infamous tragedy. The FID was branded forever with negative monikers such as USS *Zippo*, USS *Forest Fire*, and *L Zippo*, after the tragedy, and they lasted until the day she was decommissioned; in fact, some still remember her as such even today. But with that said, the United States Navy and its sailors turned what was a national tragedy into something special by simply sharing the truth of what really happened that day. The Naval Photographic Center even made a training film out of it that became a staple and mandated requirement for US Navy recruits, and millions of US sailors have watched it at all of the US Navy Recruit Training Commands (past and present), as it is known by all sailors as *Trial by Fire: A Carrier Fights for Life*

(1973). "Learn or Burn, Baby, Learn or Burn." https://www.youtube.com/watch?v=U6NnfRT_OZA

The best practices learned from the USS *Forrestal CV-59* tragedy of 1967 were invaluable to generations of firemen, seamen, airmen, construction men, and aviators alike. The sailors of the 1967 tragedy modeled what men do to move forward after horrific tragedy regardless of mishaps due to human error or otherwise. Their courage and their success under fire transcends the seas as it has also motivated triple threat special operators when they are on land, who eventually are confronted with the anxiety and uncertainty of combat operations. I am sure many of the heroic actions that they exhibited with outstanding success are a direct reflection of what the FID sailors of the 1967 tragedy did correctly.

Moreover, in today's US Navy, the best practices learned most likely have been expanded upon. But with that prime example of superior leadership under fire to follow, what happened to the plat lens footage from the January 15, 1978, tragedy? Why is it so difficult for the general public to discover just simple pictures (just one) or any authentic footage of what happened on that brisk January evening during our workups, that is, training operations, off the coast of St. Augustine, Florida? Is there such thing as a top-secret operation during training missions or what? So if not, then who was the pilot? Was it the Executive Officer of VA-81, an Attack Squadron comprised of A-7 aircraft that were assigned to Air Wing CVW-17? You know, we have always suspected him of being the culprit back then, some forty years ago, and even maybe many others in addition to me in the here and now today. Did he land on the flight deck without authorization? Why did he do it, and again, why has his name never been revealed? What about the collateral damage it has caused so many lives, families, children, moms, dads, sisters, brothers, relatives, and other loved ones? How about those individuals who have lived lifetimes of pain and suffering as they eventually became addicted, surrendering to chronic alcoholism and other substances that consumed them to the point that they became victims again, exacerbating their maladaptive behaviors, which for some have contributed to homelessness , incarceration, and in the worst case scenarios, even murder or suicide? These are the reasons why this book had to be written, for the lives that were lost, for the men who were injured physically, emotionally, and psychologically, in addition to the careers that ended, and again for the numerous families negatively affected as a result of human error, equipment malfunction, or a total disregard for human life. But with all that in question, was it a calculated and callous military cover-up, just to save some individual's or a individuals' military career? https://en.wikipedia.org/wiki/1967_USS_Forrestal_fire

Introduction

I am Wesley E. Etheridge Sr., a retired US Naval Master Trainer, author, award-winning curriculum developer, and the "Leading Authority on Military Veterans and Anger Management." A former shipmate of mine, Mr. John Pugioti, whom I had not seen since January 15, 1978, and I have collaborated and wrote this book to share his amazing story via a compare and contrast format for the primary purpose of educating the military and the general public about a horrific aircraft mishap that occurred during a point in time in both of our military careers. In addition, we share what transpired for both of us prior to and after the mishap and how it contributed to social, emotional and other dynamics for the remainder of our lives. This true story is based in part upon finding out what really happened during a tragic aircraft mishap on the flight deck of the USS Forrestal CV-59. This little-known, compelling, real-life story transpired over thirty-eight years ago, and it was the last time John and I saw each other, until September 2015, at the James J. Peters VA Medical Center located at 130 W. Kingsbridge Road, Bronx, New York. Included in this book also are some written eyewitness accounts from other sailors (shipmates) who were there that evening almost forty years ago. There eyewitness individual written accounts are as accurate as each individual could recall at the time of their writings regarding that tragic incident that, again, occurred almost forty years ago. The surviving individuals who shared in writing what they saw that evening include: Airmen Jessie Lopez and Jeffery A. West, who at that time were both assigned to *Forrestal*'s Air Department V-1 Division, and Air Wing CVW-17 Airman Paul L. Cobble, a "Brown shirt" and plan captain who was assigned to Anti Submarine Squadron VS-30. As an added "bonus" we included best practices to get the attention of legislators on Capitol Hill in addition to a suggested methodology that you or others can utilize the "WEE Concept" that has proven to be a highly successful strategy for passionate individuals who practice it, because they have grown to understand the value of discovering themselves in part, so that they can better manage the secondary emotion of anger.

From my clearest military recollection, when I last observed John, he was lying severely (gravely, in my mind) injured on the flight deck in the Fly-2 area, outside the foul line, and screaming, "My legs! My legs! I can't play basketball anymore!" hysterically and in shock just moments after completing his final re-spot. I often thought about John over the past three and a half decades, as I could never forget what happened to him that evening; I always wondered what kind of quality of life he may have had in comparison to mine. This is the story written by both John and me of "My Final Re-spot."

It was during our youthful years—we were only nineteen and twenty years old—but we had what they would call today a swagger because we thought we were invincible. We were the post–Vietnam Era military, and as "Blue shirts" who worked as the flight deck crew, we were tasked with the safe movement of million-dollar aircraft in a safe and expeditious manner. There was never any hesitation or rest during workups, and to ensure that the planes kept flying, we worked in crews and would take alternate turns for chow; taking the initiative and among ourselves we decided who would go to chow first during flight operations.

On that fateful chilly Sunday January evening, John told me to go to chow first. Little did we know that his decision would forever change the dynamics of our two lives forever? Little did we know that not only would it be John's last re-spot but maybe it would be the final one for a number of others in our ship's company air department, and our carrier air wing CVW-17.

Our story is about death, tragedy, pain, trauma, post-traumatic stress disorder, post-traumatic stress, moral injury trauma, bitterness, anger, rage, disappointment, triumph, love, forgiveness, patience, blessings, resiliency, and the power of God Almighty to heal, delivered via brotherhood and comradeship. Our story had to be told.

1

Two Towns,
Two Military Families

Born and raised in Tidewater and the city of Portsmouth, which today is known as Hampton Roads, Virginia, I (Wesley Eric Etheridge Sr.) was born in one of the nation's oldest military hospitals, Portsmouth Naval Hospital, on a Friday morning, November 15, 1957. Both of my parents were from small towns in North Carolina. My mother (Mabel) for the majority of her young adulthood was a wife, and my dad (Wassee Etheridge) was a steward (cook) in the United States Navy during the Cuban Missile Crisis and the Viet Nam era.

Etheridge family: dad and mom Gennett, Wayne, Robin, Michele, Wesley

As a member of the baby boomer generation, my two sisters and I (I was the middle child) grew up during one of the most tumultuous times in United States and world history, during the late '50s through the midway point of the '70s, or what many politicians and military service members from that era would identify as the Cold War and the Vietnam War or Conflict eras.

The basis of my childhood education outside of my Portsmouth elementary education included two other schools within the city of Portsmouth, Virginia, educational system, which included: William E. Waters Middle School and Manor High School. My mother, Mabel Virginia (Porter), lacked a formal education, and due to the fact that she was such a young wife and mother during an era when mothers valued opinions of local educators, doctors, and individuals in positional authority, she was advised to hold me back when I was a first grader—which she did—and as a result, I graduated from Manor High in 1976, a year behind my peers.

In 1975, while I was a junior in high school, I became a father, and my first son was born: Wesley Arron Etheridge Richardson. My son's mother, Sherrie Richardson, had recently relocated to the city of Portsmouth with her mother and only brother from Brooklyn, New York. Mrs. Richardson, Sherrie's mother, insisted that Sherrie and I get married, but when I informed her of my intentions, which were to graduate from high school first and immediately enlist in the military, she eventually compromised, but later changed her mind and moved them back to New York with her. Determined to do what I said, I stayed in school, got a job at J. H. Miles Oyster Company in the Ghent section of Norfolk, until graduation in June 1976 when I then promptly enlisted in the United States Navy via the delayed entry program, and eventually it was "goodbye, delayed entry program" and hello, train ride from Richmond to the Recruit Training Command, Orlando, Florida, in September 1976.

The culture shock of boot camp was the first real challenge for me as an eighteen-year-old. I soon learned the meaning of structure and discipline. I became more focused and confident, while at the same time I learned about cultures other than mine and began questioning, comparing, and reevaluating myself in comparison to others' communities, cultures, ethnicities, and personalities. Changes in the new environment were real and evident to me, especially with music, as I learned and got used to not hearing cultural favorites such as:

> Tear the roof off the sucker;
> Tear the roof off the mother sucker,
> Tear the roof off the sucker,
> 'cause we want the funk.

These lyrics were sung by Parliament Funkadelic[1] a progressive and highly talented p-funk band of musicians whose members openly smoked pot or marijuana on stage, mimicked Sir Nose, devoid of funk and others, but marched to the beat of their leader, Mr. George Clinton and his band, Mother Ship Connection. Other artists I listened to during that time included the Stylistics, Con Function, Roy Ayers, Black Birds, Grover Washington Jr., and so on.

However, at Recruit Training Command Orlando Florida, I was not the only one who arrived there after being raised on and enjoying a certain genre of music. Because thousands of other recruits did hear and listen to music in the morning also after being awaken in their racks and barracks to the sound of steel garbage cans being thrown across the barracks or berthing areas, only to hear them come crashing down on the deck and then loudly continuing to traumatize unsuspecting recruits as they began rolling down the cement and tiled decks. Unfortunately for us , this was every morning between 3:00 and 4:00 a.m., in preparation to start the day, and the start of the routine of being marched to the chow hall at what is called in the military as "0" dark "thirty" (5:30 a.m.) in military formation.

As always, there would be a fresh aroma of greasy bacon in the air;

---

1   Parliament (Musical group). 1993. *Tear the Roof Off, 1974–1980*. New York, NY: Casablanca.

recruits and assigned civilians who worked in the galley on the base could all hear the music being piped over the speakers every morning. It was Top 40 songs, classics such as:

> Someone's knocking at the door, who that's ringing the bell,
> Some one's knocking at the door, who that's ringing the bell,
> Do me a favor open the door and let them in . . .

That's the beautiful 1976 classic by Paul McCarty and Wings; there were other songs also, such as:

> Early one Sunday morning, breakfast was on the table,
> There was no time to eat;
> Mom said to me, "Boy, hurry to Sunday school . . . [2]

Those are a few lyrics from the song called "Sadie," a Top 40 hit by the Spinners, a popular crossover group.

Because my oldest sister, Gennett, was an enlisted Airman in the United States Air Force and stationed at Lakeland Airbase in the state of Florida, she attended my Pass and Review at Orlando's Recruit Training Command Graduation, for which I was very appreciative, and after a short few days of visiting with her, it was off to Lakehurst, New Jersey (commonly called Snake Hurst by ABs) to Aviation Boatswains Mate "A" School in December of 1976.

Lakehurst, New Jersey, is close to the state of New York and adjacent to what was then Fort Dix (US Army Base), which is in close proximity to Toms River, New Jersey. The Naval Air Station continues to be famous for the crash of the Zeppelin Hindenburg, a German Airship filled with over seven million cubic feet of combustible hydrogen that crashed while landing on May 6, 1937, at Naval Air Station Lakehurst, New Jersey, and killed thirty-five people.[3]

---

2   Spinners (Musical group: US). 1993. *The Very Best of Spinners*. Los Angeles, CA: Rhino.
3   Grossman, Dan. "The Hindenburg Disaster." Airships.net A Dirigible and Zeppelin History Site RSS. 2009. Accessed May 20, 2015.

Six months prior to my reporting aboard the USS *Forrestal CV-59* and subsequently being assigned to Air Department V-1 Division in early January 1977, USS *Forrestal CV-59* the world's first super carrier (affectionately nicknamed the FID after its motto: First In Defense) was part of the Navy's Annual 4th of July Fleet Week celebration, and she had a port visit that accommodated thousands of sailors in New York's Hudson River, in addition to having countless visitors from New York, its surrounding areas, and the globe. At that time, also locally, in close proximity to the iconic super carrier, was an aspiring potential New York visitor, an enlisted sailor in the United States Navy who was in the process of transitioning to the FID as his new duty station, and his name was Airman John Pugioti.

John Pugioti was born in Brooklyn New York, on December 10, 1958. He is the youngest child of three conceived by Mr. and Mrs. John Nicholas Pugioti. John's father enlisted in the United States Navy during WWII. His Sea service consisted of several hostile engagements in a variety of hostilities across the European Mediterranean during that era. As a member of the "Greatest Generation" (according to Tom Brokaw's Book with the same title) he also learned to cook during the war, and upon being honorable discharged he purchased a home and also utilized his military experience, knowledge and education to work for Nabisco Foods in New York for over forty years.

John's mother, Mrs. Rosalie Pugioti, worked with small children at a day care center and enjoyed being a loving and nurturing housewife. John grew up with his two older sisters, Elaine, the oldest child, and Karen, the middle sibling.

John's mom, dad, and daughter (Harlowe) at her sweet sixteen celebration

John was a charismatic and energetic young man as he grew up in the Overing Avenue section of the Bronx in New York, and according to his peers, he was an outstanding athlete; he really excelled at playing basketball, and he loved the game. Growing up, as a teenager and prior to joining the United States Navy, John stayed in a fair amount of trouble, hanging out with Mike and the gang, which included Lil Mike, Brian, and Mike Casey; they called themselves the Overing Boys, and like most young men growing up in a tough environment, they always seemed to be in the mix of the current or past drama within their neighborhood.

Television shows that depicted wholesome lifestyles in America, such as *Happy Days*, and other programs such as *Little House on the Prairie*, *Three's Company*, and *The Love Boat*, were regular shows on the air during that time. Though they were very popular shows during that era they were not remotely similar to the type of lifestyle John and his peers lived. In fact, their style was completely at the opposite end of the spectrum.

When John joined the United States Navy, it wasn't because of an affinity toward the US Navy or the military; it was done because his dad gave him no options. But while John's dad did encourage him to join the military, he also was resistant about the idea of him joining the United States Marine Corps, which was John's first choice. His dad, John Nicolas Pugioti, had realized that John was not interested in attending school as much as he enjoyed hanging out doing all the wrong things with his chosen group of friends, the Overing Boys.

The year was then 1976, and the Bicentennial celebration for the United States of America was potentially exciting for many, for a variety of capitalistic reasons, so patriotism was displayed everywhere as Americans celebrated two hundred years of independence from the United Kingdom. The people of the United States had little confidence in their elected GOP officials because of the Watergate scandal; hence, with the election of a Democratic president, Mr. Jimmy Carter became the nation's next president, but the transition of power from the Republican president, Mr. Gerald R. Ford, would not occur until the following year. Inflation was a global problem; the US annual rate was 5.7, while the UK annual inflation rate was 16.5 percent; gas in the US was .59 cents per gallon, while in the UK it was 0.76 British pounds.[4]

---

4   "The Year 1976 from the People History." What Happened in 1976 Including Pop Culture, Prices, Events and Technology. Accessed May 22, 2015.

Further, in world politics, James Callaghan became Britain's prime minister; Mao Tse-tung, founder of the Chinese Communist Party died; and Fidel Castro became the president of Cuba. In Montreal, Canada, the Olympics were being held but the event was boycotted by thirty-two black African Nations.[5] The Bicentennial year saw the expansion of technology with the birth of Apple Computers, formed by Steve Jobs and Steve Wozniak, and the United States space craft's Viking I & II settled down safely on Mars. The Concord entered service and cut transatlantic flying time to three and a half hours, and even though it was a very festive atmosphere, nationwide terror began on the streets of New York when the Son of Sam began his series of attacks terrorizing New Yorkers and their families.

During the Bicentennial celebration weekend, which included the 4th of July, 1976, the USS *Forrestal CV-59* was the host for the International Naval Review in New York City. From the *Forrestal's* flight deck, President Gerald Ford rang in the nation's Bicentennial and reviewed over forty tall ships from countries all over the world. The celebration on the Hudson River also allowed for active duty sailors to enjoy liberty call in one of the most beloved cities in the nation and the world.

As stated earlier, John was home in transition from the Navy during that summer. He had two weeks of leave before he was to report to the USS *Forrestal CV-59* for duty. Shortly after completing Boot Camp at Recruit Training Command Great Lakes, Illinois, in the early months of 1976, John got orders that same year to attend Aviation Electronic Tech School in Memphis, Tennessee. However, it was short-lived because within several weeks John began having difficulties academically and eventually rocked out. It was not because of his behavior or his understanding of the materials; it was because of his lack of a foundation in regards to understanding the fundamentals of algebra. During that educational era in America, it was not a mandated requirement for high school students to take

---

5   Wikipedia contributors, "1976 Summer Olympics," *Wikipedia, The Free Encyclopedia,* http://en.wikipedia.org/w/index.php?title=1976_Summer_Olympics&oldid=662769370 (accessed May 20, 2015).

algebra (it was an elective); therefore, many high school students in the inner cities chose not to take it, and for many years later, it would came back to haunt many students of that era.

On July 16, 1976 Airman John Pugioti arrived in the Tidewater area and reported aboard the USS Forrestal CV-59 at the Norfolk Naval Shipyard in Portsmouth, Virginia, where the ship was beginning rehabilitation—a normal routine after a major deployment and part of the normal eighteen-month cycle that extends the life of a US Navy aircraft carrier. Upon arrival, John was assigned to Air Department V-1 Division. Almost immediately he was temporarily assigned to duty (TAD), cleaning various officers' quarters for a routine ninety-day span.

In the early days of January 1977, I also arrived at yard in Portsmouth, Virginia, carrying my sea bag with pride and high expectations as I arrived from Aviation Boatswains Mate School in Lakehurst, New Jersey. A native of Portsmouth, Virginia, and recent 1976 graduate of Manor High School, as discussed earlier, I reported onboard the USS Forrestal CV-59, just two weeks after my first cousin Eddie J. Scarbough, received his honorable discharge and got out of the Navy. He was an undesignated seamen and boat coxswain assigned to Deck dept., on the FID. Because my cousin was a former squid on the "FID" it subsequently made me have an added sense of pride for being assigned to Air Department's V-1 Division.

Needless to say, one of the worst things that could happen to a young black male who was born and raised down South in the 1970s was that he could get arrested and have something happen to him while in custody; he could come up missing because of racial prejudices or get killed on the street either by consuming illicit narcotics—which were prevalent on the streets, especially after the Vietnam era—or by being murdered by another African American because he was at the wrong place at the wrong time.

Because of the lack of viable options, I understood that, as the father of an infant child, the only way I could get an opportunity to take care of him was to become a military service member. However, I never realized that there would be consequences for joining a branch of the service that would send me to Boot Camp—an "A" school in Lakehurst, New Jersey—and assign me literally at home in my own backyard.

As a wide-eyed, immature, and naive young sailor in my hometown, I was constantly running into individuals I went to school with who did not believe I was in the military. After all, graduation was in June 1976, and by early 1977 I was back in the area. I had first cousins all on my mother's side of the family who lived in the Douglas Park area in Portsmouth, Norfolk's Campestella Heights and the Projects (a subsidized residential dwelling) in the Liberty Park area, which was close to the downtown Scope arena, Norfolk State College, and Diggs Park, which were all located in Norfolk across the water from Portsmouth. I was thrilled (and naive) in thinking that because the USS *Forrestal* CV-59 was home ported i.e., stationed in Portsmouth where I was primarily raised was a blessing for me, but in reality, it was a huge liability. I guess it was inevitable that I would eventually spend most of my off-duty liberty time in the city of Portsmouth downtown area at a project residential area called Ida Barbour. There I had some of my favorite cousins on my dad's side of the family—Kenneth, also known as Hank, and Dennis, his little brother, along with one of their older brothers who also was an enlisted United States Navy sailor, who eventually retired as a Gunners mate, Chief Sterling Marshall.

By midyear 1977, the USS *Forrestal* CV-59 began sea trials and work-ups in preparation for its upcoming Mediterranean deployment, which was scheduled to begin on April 4, 1978. However, at that time, the crew also found out that it was changing homeports from Pier 12 of the Norfolk Naval Shipyard to Naval Station Mayport, Florida—in other words, Jacksonville—which meant Duval County and its beautiful white sandy beaches.

The mixed emotions, immaturity, and excitement of knowing that the ship was relocating to another home port and would finally get me away from home (one of the reasons I enlisted) became an excuse for me to listen more to my cousins in Portsmouth than my supervisors onboard the FID. I began spending more time smoking pot with them and becoming oblivious to the fact that they were going nowhere fast with their limited knowledge and education. Thus, I was swayed by them so much, to the point that they convinced me to spend the last two weeks absent without leave (AWOL) before the ship loaded up the flight deck and hanger bay with the twenty-four hundred ship crew members (no Air Wing Squadron personnel) and our vehicles in preparation for relocation to the ship's new home port in beautiful Mayport, Florida.

As the ship was preparing to get underway, I finally came to my senses and returned to the USS *Forrestal CV-59 the day before we got underway*. Upon my return, the ship got underway and was at sea for approximately thirteen days, and it was during this time that I had to face the consequences of my actions, which entailed non-judicial punishment (NJP) on the Bridge with the *Forrestal*'s commanding officer, Captain Peter B. Booth. When questioned by the commanding officer as to why I went AWOL, as an immature and young nineteen-year-old, I remember stating (demonstrating that I indeed was clueless), "I don't know." Luckily for me the commanding officer knew from looking at my service record that I was a kid and was most likely influenced by my friends and family members in my home town. Therefore, the captain stated, "Because you work on the flight deck, which is a very demanding laborious job in itself, and because I hear from your superiors that you are a hard worker, I am awarding you fourteen days restriction starting today and a $100 fine."

The good thing was that my captain's mast (non- judicial punishment) was on the first day at sea, and the USS *Forrestal CV-59* was scheduled to pull into its new home port in Mayport, Florida, on the thirteenth day. It also meant that I would be a spectator observing from either the flight deck or the hanger bay the day of arrival. In essence, just being an observer of the live marching band playing the home port celebratory music, which also included the United States Navy's favorite song, "Anchors Away," *in* addition to eyeballing other sailors as they would meet all the single women who would be welcoming the FID and its sailors to their new home port. Thus, when we docked in Mayport for the initial time, I would be coerced to remain on the flight deck and observe all the fanfare from there, because I still had one day of restriction remaining on the ship as a consequence of being AWOL, or what some others may call UA or unauthorized absence. In addition, I was $100 lighter in my wallet; at this point in my life, yes, I was a follower and definitely not yet a leader.

2

Life Onboard a US Naval Aircraft Carrier in the Portsmouth Naval Shipyard

Life in the shipyard, or the "yards," as US sailors, naval shipyard workers, and others working on the base or private yard would called it, was and is a grind. Can you picture civilian contractors competing to secure government contracts worth millions and billions of dollars, in addition to the many possibilities for contracted workers to travel around the world as consultants, assisting with repair or preventative maintenance on anyone of America's most powerful military weapons—including prestigious United States aircraft carriers?

During that time, when we served onboard, the repair and maintenance on the FID was the responsibility of the Norfolk Naval Shipyard in Portsmouth and Norfolk Virginia. The reason a carrier or any United States military vessel goes into a yard period is for repair and or preventative maintenance. This also includes upgrading of state-of-the-art technological systems and equipment as well as allowing time for training new crew members because the vessel would usually be returning from a major deployment, which would systematically necessitate a high turnover of seasoned personnel and provide an opportunity to again repair, update, or add nomenclature or components that ensure the combat vessels fighting edge over our enemy.

In fact, from my perspective, a perfect analogy would be that of a sports team getting new players in all positions who understand the basics of their craft, but they have to become familiar with a new system while discovering true chemistry in order to assist the team to win. In the case of the military, regarding winning (again, from my perspective), we are talking about what equates to accomplishing the mission in the most efficient and expeditious manner at the most economical cost, while sustaining zero or a minimal loss of US military lives. During the yard period, many divisions sent most of their sailors on temporary assigned duty (TAD), especially the Air Department, because frankly, airmen had very limited amounts of other responsibilities if the ship did not have aircraft onboard, or if they were not re-spotting, launching, recovering, fueling, or refueling United States military aircraft.

Yes, the sailors in V-1 Division had some primary duties and responsibilities that they were required to do, but they had to obligate upward to approximately (and I am guessing) sixty percent of their manpower to other areas of the ship while in the yards to ensure that the proper attention was being given to the rehabilitation of the ship itself. Supervisors ensured that they kept their best workers who had already proven themselves as outstanding ABs while they were on the previous deployment as well as various other blue-water or underway sea times. While others were sent TAD, for those who remained with the division the carefully hand-selected skeleton crew (a term for a limited amount of available manpower) worked half days and had plenty of extra days off. When they put their time in, they worked diligently and they lived up to the AB (Aviation Boastewainsmate) reputation of working hard and playing hard. They rehabbed all compartments that were the responsibility of V-1 Division.

On every carrier ABs ensure that they are counted as all in, by drawing and painting (in bright yellow) a huge set of AB Wings on the forward side of the Island structure, in fact on May 1, 2003 you can see the world famous AB Wings behind then President George W. Bush as he is on the flight deck of the USS Abraham Lincoln (CVN-72), when he announced that major combat operations in Iraq had ended. Also, if you observe the YouTube video regarding Mission Accomplished at: https://youtu.be/5BIW6qyrdu4 you can see the AB Wings as Mr. George W. Bush walks to the podium. Simultaneously you shall also see on the starboard side of him the multi colored flight deck jerseys which were part of the photo op, for that controversial event. It also shows the results of a rehabbed flight deck Island structure and 04 level which required AB's to be adept at utilizing an assortment of standard shipyard pneumatic hand tools: i.e., needle guns, knuckle busters, deck crawlers, paint pods, sprayers, specialized sand blasters, and other equipment to grind, peel up, and sand-surface rust prior to priming and painting all marine nomenclature and surfaces. A lot of pride goes into meticulously completing the resurfacing and non-skidding of large portions of the flight deck's surfaces including abrasive and non-abrasive areas in the Fly-3 landing area, the Fly-2 six pack and the alley where the E-2 Hawkeye would normally be spotted while underway, Fly-1's bow area, and an assortment of weather decks both on the port (left) and starboard (right) sides of the ship adjacent to the catwalks.

Additionally, they performed all other required tasks, which demonstrated why they were top-notch sailors and shipmates, which included: collateral duties such as standing berthing watch, quarter deck, or after brow watch and being part of the ship's in-port duty rotation, which may have included being a team leader or member of the ship's emergency fire squad, and performing mass casualty and fire drill training on every duty day (normally a six day rotation , in our day) just in case a fire broke out while the ship was in the yards. As for those who were TAD and not part of the skeleton crew while the FID was in the yards, many put in long days, had structured hours, aggressive supervision, and strict accountability to adhere to. We were in the dry dock—in our situation; the FID basically was on bricks in a controlled area (akin to you sitting in a bathtub with your buttocks sitting or resting on supports above the bottom of a waterless tub) that may or may not be filled with water depending on the maintenance situation of the type of vessel in the dry dock. The bottom line is that a dry dock is a place where a marine vessel rests off the deck (with no water) while in the yards so that there can be a comprehensive set of maintenance tasks and inspections performed on the hull or underneath the vessel in addition to other, and I am sure confidential, secret, and top secret actions that ensure seaworthiness, watertight integrity, and so forth. This maintenance process is strategically and specifically designed to extend the life of the vessel by being proactive in regards to repairs that also include scheduled and unscheduled maintenance.

During this era in the late '70s, the eighteen-month maintenance cycles scheduled for all *Forrestal* class carriers consisted of six months of practice, preferably blue-water ops over brown water ops (blue water ops means you see water as far as the eye can see, brown water you are closer to land), launching, recovering, re-spotting, and fueling and refueling aircraft, which is commonly called work-ups (like the pre-season in sports), then ideally six months (but sometimes, depending on world events or other unforeseen events it can be up to nine or more) of overseas deployment, which culminates with six months of scheduled overhaul maintenance—unless the ship had major mechanical challenges, which may cause her to be in the yards period longer than expected. If that was the case, then the ship's commanding officer or CO, would more than likely end up with a serious challenge in regards to career advancement to become Admiral.

For individuals who were sent packing or those on a temporary duty assignment (TAD), here is a list of what some ninety-day assignments consisted of: assignments to the engineering department (hating life) working below the engineer's deck plates, fire watch (boring twelve-hour shifts watching civilians weld, your task is to ensure nothing catches on fire and when authority was not looking; finding a place to smoke a joint or two, but usually not alone and maybe with the welder himself (as we assimilated to behaviors associated with the post Vietnam era), ships rehab (ripping out components or partitions and replacing them), or off the ship either in the naval station galley or mess hall (mess duties), base security (pass and ID), bachelors enlisted quarters (BEQ), or bachelors officers quarters (BOQ), cleaning, standing watch, et cetera. In nearly 100 percent of the situations, if you were one of the new Airmen Recruits E-1 through E-3 reporting from ABH "A" school from Lakehurst, New Jersey, or any other place, you did not have a choice in where they sent you for TAD.

John on his bike in 1977 adjacent to Norfolk Naval Aircraft Carrier Pier

Luckily for John, he was temporarily assigned to duty cleaning various officers' quarters. Any sailor who has been a part of ship's company for an extended period of time and had been in the yards before certainly understood that being assigned TAD to anything that had the officers country attached to it was a pleasurable opportunity, a skate, or an easy job for whomever was assigned to it. Understanding that he had time to do it, John took advantage of this opportunity and earned his GED as he began to think about advancement and understood that even though he did not complete high school in the Bronx of New York, he was more than capable of earning his GED.

Several other airmen from the air department and I were assigned temporary duty with the dreaded engineering department. In particular, I was assigned to one of the hottest places to work (and I am not talking about women), which required crawling on my belly in a moist, greasy, and foul odor crawl space area that was underneath the machinery room deck plates in order to use pneumatic needle guns, knuckle busters, grinders, and sanders which were the necessary tools needed to prep these areas prior to priming them with red lead (an absolute necessity that enhances preservation for steel surfaces) before we painted the deck below the deck plates itself.

One morning after two other young sailors (airmen) and I had gathered our safety goggles, ear protectors, and gloves and were preparing to perform our daily refurbishing task in the bilge of a machinery room that we were assigned to refurbish by a Third-Class Petty Officer Hull Technician, one of the other sailors (airmen) decided that he was going to refuse to work and needle gun that morning and in fact he verbally expressed his intentions to the Third-Class Petty Officer by stating with some explicit words, such as, "#@&! This!" As he threw his needle gun on the deck inside the crawl space area in which he was told to crawl and refurbish. Seconds later, the Petty Officer Third Class authoritatively told him to come with him, and the young sailor boasted In a clear baritone bolsterous manner something to the effect of "Hey, I'll go with you," as my colleague who was an airmen (undesignated ABH) from V-3 Division, and I watched (his name was Cherokee) in amazement for his disdain for authority, we also promptly looked at each other in astonishment and with a degree of anxiety in regards to what was going to happen next as we both stood frozen in time at a standstill in the same exact work area. But then, in what seemed like seconds later, (at least from my perspective) the young sailor promptly ran back to his assigned area at our location, jumped into the crawl space (and I am sure before his feet could hit the deck) immediately grabbed his needle gun and without hesitation or making any eye contact with either of us, he began needle gunning without another word said.

It was at this time that both Cherokee (who was named such because he was a Caucasian-looking fellow lean and tall—easily over six feet with blond hair and blue eyes—but he was a proud Cherokee Indian from Cherokee, North Carolina, and he wanted everyone to respect who and what he was, more than anything) and I looked each other in the eyes, smiled, laughed, and then with a renewed vigor and appreciation for respect, we continued completing our assigned task. I have never forgotten this incident, because it was my first real lesson learned (outside of boot camp) regarding leadership in the United States Navy.

After both John and I completed our TAD time, we returned to our primary responsibilities with Air Department V-1 Division. We both eventually ended up working for Fly-3 Petty Officer, Yellow Shirt, and Aircraft Director ABH-**2** Jessie Puente, a Texas native who was married and had a family. We also were under the tutelage and supervision of Yellow Shirt Assistant Fly-3 PO Johnny Gill, a career-minded sailor also; I believe Johnny was a Kentucky native who had a fiancée and less than a couple of months remaining regarding his tour on the FID.

USS FORRESTAL (CV-59) PATCH

To be completely honest, even though John was a year younger, he was more mature and focused. He understood and had a game plan for moving up the ladder of success in the division more rapidly than most of us at the time. He was from the Bronx and had gotten away from home, which allowed him to mature faster and reflect more on his future than his immediate situation, while on the other hand, I was stationed in my hometown a mere ten-minute drive from the Portsmouth Naval Ship Yard to my parents' home in the Cavalier Manor section of the city, which contributed to a delay in maturity and a lack of career focus.

3

Workups, Haze Gray, and Underway

Air Department, which was considered V-O Division, was reserved primarily for the intellectual administrative individuals, so-called nerds and pencil or paper pushers. In short, if the ship was at sea or underway, its assigned personnel would be distinguished by wearing white turtleneck shirts (we called them jerseys) with four-inch letters, "VO" stenciled on the front and back of each individual's flight deck jersey and individual float coat in large black letters, similar to numbers on an athlete's jersey in sports.

The department was primarily responsible for all of the executive administrative duties for the ship's air department; it would be akin to the air department headquarters at a military airfield or a civilian airport. It was headed by the ship's Air Boss and Mini-Boss who could wear any color jersey they liked; however they often, more times than not, chose to wear yellow. Sailors assigned to VO were nicknamed Tower Flowers because they worked exclusively in the air-conditioned confines of primary flight control, or Pri-Fly, which was the designated name for the highest and supposedly one of the safest locations on the ship from which to observe the launching, recovery and re-spot of aircraft on the carrier itself, sort of like the Booth were an NFL commentator would view and comment on the game he was analyzing on, with the exception that the Boss (Air Boss) called the plays or the shots. Nicknames derived from military acronyms were a prominent part of the dynamics and culture in which masculine-minded individuals (who held positional authority based upon military structure) rationalized that enlisted personnel assigned to VO division would be selected to work there because of stereotypical reasons, such as an assumed lack of courage, toughness, and being observed as one who was lacking in physical statue or masculinity based upon one's appearance and even how they articulated. Basically, this status quo methodology of thought was because it would be surmised that they most likely would not do well in a work environment that was as physically demanding as the labor-intensive dynamics that individuals who worked on the flight deck or hanger bays in V-1 to V-4 divisions would be toiling and or performing in.

Again, V-O Division, or the Air Department Office, is where the Air Boss, Mini-Boss, and other assigned or specialty personnel, who assisted with the safety and management of air operations on, off, or near the aircraft carrier, performed their assigned task in support of US Naval Aviation. In an exhibition of strength and global power on various occasions while out at sea, many dignitaries (VIPs from foreign countries, US congressmen, world-class athletes, national or international celebrities alike, etc.) were invited to observe the power, beauty, chemistry, and flawless orchestrations of a strategic and unique collection of colored jerseys worn by hundreds of dedicated young airmen dressed out in flight helmets, flight suits, flight-deck cranial's, flight-deck jerseys, and float coats as they masterfully towed, pushed by hand, moved utilizing mechanical technology, re-spotted, fueled, armed, launched and recovered dozens of military aircraft within minutes without a single aircraft mishap or incident.

John and I reported onboard the FID approximately six months apart, but we both where assigned to Air Department's V-1 Division, a division that was responsible for the safe and expeditious movement of military aircraft, but for us at that time, it was exclusively on the flight deck of the FID. If the ship was at sea or underway, Air Departments

V-1 and V-3 assigned personnel would be exclusively distinguished by each individual sailor (airman) wearing one of the following colored turtleneck jerseys, float coats, or vests with specialty words or lettering stenciled on the fronts and backs. That said, each individual color and job responsibility would be as follows:

1) **Yellow shirts**: for flight and hanger deck supervisors. Ideally they would be at a minimum a Third Class Petty Officer thus they are commonly referred to as "Petty Officers" but in certain situations maturity could supersede or take precedence and a senior airmen could wear the prestigious "Yellow' shirt, and this could happen on either the flight deck (responsible for Fly-1, 2, and 3), which would be V-1 Division, or in the hanger bay (responsible for Bays 1, 2, and 3), which would be V-3 Division. Even though they are always in competition to make rank (advancement), the personnel assigned to V-1 and V 3 Divisions were designated Aviation Boatswain's Mates Handlers, or ABH; therefore, they had to wear stenciled yellow shirts with the corresponding designation of "Fly-1," "Fly-2," or "Fly-3" for V-1 Division, or if they were assigned to the hanger bay, which was V-3 Division, their jerseys and individual flotation devices (vests) would say "Bay 1," "2," or "3" on them.

Likewise, in the case of Senior or Junior Officers or ultimate positional authority, their jerseys and float coats or vests would be yellow and stenciled: "Commanding Officer," "Air Boss," "Mini-Boss," "Flight Deck Officer,""Assistant Flight Deck Officer", "Hanger Bay Officer" , "Assistant Hanger Bay Officer" or "Aircraft Handling Officer," according to their positional authority.

2) **Blue shirts:** stenciled with the designation of "Fly-1," "Fly-2," or "Fly-3" or in case of a supervisor who worked as the Tractor King "TK" or the assistant (often called Tractor Queen), "TQ" or any recognizable symbol that would designate them as such would be stenciled on the front and back of their flight deck jersey, including float coat. It would be similar (with the exception of Bays) on both the flight deck and hanger bay. It also would be applicable to the Elevator Operator supervisors and all Elevator Operators because they wore blue.

Elevator Operator's wore Blue shirts also; Jeffery West is the operator you see here

3) **Red shirts**: stenciled with the designation "Crash and Salvage" on them or in the case of a supervisor: "Crash and Salvage Officer," "Crash Senior Chief Petty Officer," "Chief Petty Officer" or "Crash and Salvage Leading Petty Officer" or "LPO." In V-3 Division, which is on the hanger bay/deck area, ABH's may wear red shirts or jerseys, which may designate them as members of the ship's damage control team; in either situation, the color designates firefighting with the exception of other rates working on the flight deck or hanger bay for example a "BB" stacker, which is a nick name or moniker for Aviation Ordnanceman or AO, they handled ordnance , bombs and thing associated with munitions.

4) **Green shirts**: stenciled with the designation "Arresting Gear" or "Cats", depending on if they worked on the aft end of the carrier, or on the waist or bow area. In which case they may have a large "A" or the words Arresting Gear printed on their jersey or a image of a wild cat with the word "Cat" (short for catapults), and in the case of being

a supervisor, recognizable lettering that would designate them as such would be stenciled on the front and back of their flight deck jersey or float coat. In the case of ultimate positional authority, their jersey and float coat would read "V-2 Division Officer," "Bow Officer," "Arresting Gear Officer" or "Waist Cat Officer." Again, Officers would be designated according to which area on the flight deck or catapult they were assigned to, either catapults 1 or 2 if they worked on the forward area of the flight deck or catapults 3 or 4 if they worked on the angled deck portion of the flight deck (waist cats), which is parallel to the ship's island structure on all United States Navy aircraft carriers. Similarly it would be the same for Arresting Gear Officers.

In summary, they worked on the flight deck on all aircraft carriers. Managing and operating all catapults and the arresting gear which is located in the Fly-3 area, or the aft end of the ship. The gear area (short for "arresting gear") is comprised of four arresting gear cables and an aircraft barricade, which would be erected only for training purposes, or in an actual aircraft in flight emergency landing. Candidly speaking, without the expertise of the ABE, there could be no launch or recovery of carrier based aircraft on any flight deck.

ABE's also assisted (in a limited capacity) Landing Signal Officers, or LSO's (formerly known as Paddles in the early days of Naval Aviation), they wore white jerseys with float coats with the words LSO, as their identifying designation. Primarily a responsibility of the ship's air wing, one of the LSO's primary responsibilities during flight operations (i.e., Flt., Ops.), is manning the catwalk during aircraft recovery on the port side (left) of the ship in the Fly-3 area. Some other responsibilities may have included monitoring or eyeballing height, distance, speed of aircraft, and keeping communication with incoming military aircraft as they approach the carrier for landing. This includes "Waving Off," meaning the pilot is flying too low or too high (off the ball), and he needs to be sent around to reengage into the aircraft pattern with the remaining aircraft seeking to land on the deck of the carrier. Aircraft "Waving Off" is standard operating procedure for all pilots whose aircraft approach is not congruent with the meatball for a safe, authorized, shipboard landing. Additionally, on the *Forrestal* Class Aircraft Carriers, all LSOs had use of technology called the Optical Landing System (OLS), nicknamed "the meatball" by some or "The Ball" by others, it was or is vital to assist LSO's to help all carrier pilots land (ideally) by safely landing their aircrafts via the sweet spot (center line) of the landing area of an aircraft carrier in a manner in which the tail hook of their perspective aircraft catches the number three wire and comes to an abrupt, screeching, violent, and sudden halt.

5) **Grapes, or Purple shirts**: V-4 Division the Air Department's fourth Division of Aviation Boatswains mates (ABF) worked on the fight deck and below decks. Fueling, defueling, or refueling military aircraft in addition to monitoring and managing fuel tanks containing the volatile JP-4 and JP-5 aviation fuels on all *Forrestal* class carriers. They wore shirts that were stenciled with "F" on them. Supervisors wore shirts or jerseys and float coats with the words "Fuels Chief Petty Officer," "Fuels Leading Petty Officer," or "P.O." stenciled on both the fronts and backs. In the case of ultimate positional authority, the jersey and float coat would read "V-4 Division Officer" or "Assistant Fuels Officer."

In civilian terms, military job titles are often referred to as "military occupation specialty" or "MOS." In the United States Navy, the designation Aviation Boatswains Mate, or AB, is used rather than the US Navy referring to job titles as an MOS, as they prefer to utilize the term "rate" or "rating." During our era, the AB rate was subdivided into ABH, which were the handlers; ABE, which were the equipment operators, i.e., launch and recovery specialists and the ABF, which were the aircraft fuelers; they specialized in defueling and fueling military aircraft in addition to safe handling, decontamination, and storage of all petroleum products.

On a typical air department flying day at sea, the day's flight plan typically depends on a combination of things, such as the ship's purpose or mission at sea, location at sea i.e., blue-water ops or brown water ops meaning just off the coast or land or out at sea for as far as the eye could see, number and type of aircraft onboard, decisions made by the carrier Air Wing Commander, the Commanding Officer of the carrier itself, global hot spots, and challenging situations to our nations security or our allies, etc. The flight plan would be handed down the chain of command which would include from Pri-Fly to the Aircraft Handling Officer along with the Flight Deck Officer or his assistant who also worked directly out of Flight Deck Control, located on the 04 level of the ship. Control itself i.e., Flight Deck Control could also be accessed directly from any hatch attached to the flight deck island structure or from the 03 level below, or above from the 05 level. The Handler or Aircraft Handling Officer (AHO) disseminates the flight plan and all pertinent information regarding aircraft flying movement, et cetera, to the Flight Deck Officer (who is also the V-1 Division Officer), who huddles with his Aviation Boatswains Mates and simultaneously delivers a hard copy of the day's flight schedule to those who would be executing the task of moving aircraft safely for a successful launch, recovery and re-spot for that particular cycle or phase of the carrier mission. In turn, the supervisors would share information with their subordinates in Air Dept., including CVW-17 squadron personnel (all of whom wore a variety of different colored jerseys themselves) with stenciled multicolored flight deck helmet or cranial's complete with goggles and inner ear plugs, and float coats, with high-top steel-toe flight deck boots and leather gloves, all in accordance with their designation regarding expected job performance in support of "one of the most dangerous occupations in the world."

I have to mention this also, during our era, I distinctly remember a time when I was in Flight Deck Control for a launch briefing and I overheard the AHO chuckling and stating at the same time the "Bubbas" can do it! As he was referring to the blue shirts (I was one at the time), and frankly I took immediate offense to it. Being branded by some Officer with what I believed at the time was a derogatory moniker, as he laughed at us and utilized the term "the Bubbas" just because (and this is was just my opinion at that time) we had the most undervalued and most disrespected physically demanding (and yes, not necessarily the most critically thinking) job on the flight deck. It really got under my skin and it actually motivated me to value progress and accomplishment, and it also enhanced my individual self-efficacy.

John, center right with no shirt on, with ABH-3 CJ Murphy leaning on his right shoulder

A typical day of flying could start off at 0530 in the morning with the first launch, which may consist of the launching of a variety of carrier air wing aircraft that were spotted in their position from the previous evening's final re-spot. A launch always consisted of taxiing or towing (being moved via tow bar and MD3 tow-tractor also) an aircraft via hand signals by the yellow shirt directors, but in some situations it also took lots of human manpower to push a bird (aircraft) which may have been off a spot by just a smidge while it was on a catapult or it's designated spot. In this case as many as ten or more of a variety of the flight deck crew members (exhibiting a rainbow of colors) could be observed pushing an aircraft with their bare hands, each remaining cautious as each man ideally ensured that they stayed away from the sucking power of the aircrafts high powered turning engines, which could suck a man's whole helmet or his entire body deep into its intakes, were the individual would face grave consequences including maiming or death.

A modified MD-3 Tractor with Crash and Salvage firefighting equipment attached

Multiple types of aircraft could be sent to one of the four catapults, i.e., cats, either on the bow or waist catapults for launch. The process or evolution of the launch would normally take mere minutes for approximately twenty-five aircraft to be catapulted off the deck of an aircraft carrier. The process is made possible by the aircraft catapult, which is a device designed to assist take-off of military aircraft specifically designed to be catapulted off the flight deck of aircraft carriers via a steel track built into the flight deck.

Each aircraft were carefully and expertly taxied onto the catapult by the Aviation Boatswains Mate (ABH), or Yellow shirts, precisely in a manner that allowed for the flawless execution and coordination between another type of Aviation Boatswains Mate (ABE), or Green shirt, so that they could attach the nose gear of the aircraft to a designated shuttle, so that it could be launched in an expeditious manner. Aircraft such as an A-7 Corsair, A-6 Intruder, S-3 Viking, E-2 Hawkeye or any of the various other carrier aircraft during that particular era were required to be launched off the deck in that manner. If it was a different type of aircraft, such as a F-8 Gator or a F-4 fighter jet which was affectionately called the Phantom, they would have to utilize a wire rope contraption called a catapult bridal to attach the aircraft to the ship's catapult shuttle in preparation for launch.

The catapult shuttle (with its large attached piston underneath the deck) was designed to slide on the surface of the flight deck track which facilitated the up-and-down or forward and aft sliding movement at a determined or controlled rate of speed, all movement occurred as it was propelled by the steam pressure that was being generated below the flight deck itself. Concurrently, a release bar would hold the aircraft in place until enough pressure was built up to break or release a shear pin, which freed the piston to pull the aircraft along the deck at a tremendously high rate of speed. The speed gained was equivalent to at least five times the force of gravity as it yanked the aircraft a couple of hundred feet off of the deck of the aircraft carrier forcing it to become airborne.

The formula and calculations for making each aircraft launch in this manner was determined by the aircraft's velocity, by the actions of the catapult and a host of other factors, including information gathered by the V-2 Division Catapult Officer who is the Green shirt who is actually on the deck engaged in this most important but dangerous action and the individual that you see in the movie "Top Gun" who gives the pilot a salute which signals authorization to release the aircraft for takeoff. I am sure there are others in the carrier air wing including possibly Pri-Fly who would have calculated the weight of each potential launching aircraft based upon its best practices and also the type of aircraft, the ship's speed plus or minus for that day's wind. All of this is done to ensure that the aircraft had sufficient momentum and wind underneath it to fly off the carrier deck in a safe and flawless manner. If by chance things did not go flawlessly upon takeoff, there potentially could be catastrophic results for the aircraft or ship itself, but most importantly it could be potentially deadly consequences for the crew in the aircraft and the men on the flight deck of the aircraft carrier. As one (unknown) US Naval Aviator stated long ago, "It's like being in the pocket of a slingshot under tension waiting to be shot into space like a BB."

After the safe launch and upon completion of their mission, each pilot would fly in a disciplined manner in accordance with the directives given by the Air Boss or his assistant in Pri-Fly, as each would land in a specific order that again was determined by a variety of factors that included: amount of fuel remaining in each aircraft, the ship or aircraft close proximity to a bingo station or landing area ashore, the pilot, possibly his navigator, or others' well-being, et cetera.

As somewhat stated earlier (but in a less comprehensive manner) landing on the carrier deck requires precision flying expertise, so assistance from the Fresnel Optical Lenses, which are located in the catwalk port side aft, along with the landing signal officers who in the modern-day Navy are commonly referred to as the LSO's, are heavily dependent upon by each pilot for a safe landing. For those who are nostalgic history buffs , you know that back in the early days of naval aviation history and during WWII, a lack of technology or sophistication, lead to the use of handheld paddles to signal pilots in for a safe landing; thus, they were called paddles prior to being called LSO's. However, it was much more challenging during that era to land an aircraft on an aircraft carrier than it was in the 70's and even today, simply because of modern day advanced technology like the Fresnel or Optical Lens.

After every launch and recovery of aircraft (called cycles), the same routine transpired, meaning AB's from each division, along with squadron personnel, would do their particular job. For example, the Grapes would fuel or refuel aircraft according to the flight plan in preparation for the next cycle or launch, or if it were a CVW-17 Plan Captain he would (Brown shirts) ensure final checks were completed on his aircraft or (Red shirts) ordinance men, ensured that the correct load of bomb's or munitions were available for each aircraft prior to each cycle of launch, recover, and re-spot. The same process would repeat itself over and over again all day, evening, and into the morning, or multiple days—ninety-six, seventy-two, forty-eight hours, et cetera at a time, if necessary, until the flight schedule was satisfied or the mission was complete.

There were other schedules for flying aircraft, such as Alert's, Flex Deck (of which all were different from a normal routine cycle) or Alpha Strikes when we launched everything on the flight deck in order to send every available type of CVW-17 (Carrier Air Wing Seventeen) aircraft to destroy a designated enemy target. In essence, regardless of what type of flying we did, it ultimately came down to the Re-spotting, Launching, and Recovering of aircraft at the hands of AB's.

Life on the flight deck during flight operations was as exhausting both mentally and physically as it could get. Between cycles all supervisors of crews, regardless of being in the Air Department or a member of air wing CVW -17 squadron, would ensure that their flight deck crew teams were divided into several crews in order to keep individuals alert, feed, and sharp, at their profession; an individual in a crew might possibly have worked twelve hours on and twelve hours off, or two cycles on and two cycles off, and you sneaked in a nap or chow if you could. A cycle would last approximately ninety minutes, and if you had a good crew who were able to get the aircraft in the correct spots in preparation for the next launch within forty-five minutes or less, supervisors noticed that and took it as a sign that you knew what you were doing, which led to greater positions of responsibility for you and greater prestige in the eyes of your peers, who toiled with you on the ever dangerous and unforgiving steel non-skidded abrasive and non abrasive areas of the flight deck. To further clarify, basically non-skid is a rough surface that contributes to keeping aircraft from moving about or shifting while they are secured to the flight or hanger decks.

When I say if you had a good crew, basically that would be an efficient Yellow shirt (aircraft director) or two and a couple of pairs of hustling Blue shirts with a couple of competent tractor drivers, teamwork baby; otherwise you could possibly be wasting valuable time moving just one aircraft back and forth, back and forth, and back and forth, frustratingly attempting to get that particular aircraft or even worse one of the more difficult ones to spot, on its own unique spot, which means secured on the correct spot in order to meet the Aircraft Handling Officers' (AHO) satisfaction for a potentially efficient and incident-free launch.

Again, if you were good, the crew would have a couple of minutes before the next launch to close their eyes for a few moments in the catwalk, Blue shirt hole or Yellow shirt locker room, you could also possibly have a snack or a boxed lunch (consisting of a yummy rotten apple, moldy bread, some greenish,whiteish and brown looking roast beef, (or what we sarcastically called horse cock) in between launches and cycles if there was no time to rotate to chow that day. Heck, one could smoke a cigarette or two, for those who smoked, or maybe joke with each other about something silly that happened on the deck or when you were on liberty (free time off the ship) together.

The most challenging and demanding thing about being a Blue shirt was the fact that during most launch, recovery and re-spots , you carried multiple pairs of chalks easily weighing over twelve pounds each or more depending on if they were metal or rubber coupled with a pair of tie-down chains that were usually wrapped around your neck, draping down on your chest to about stomach or waist. However during flex deck you would carry a minimum six to ten chains (twelve pounds each) and that's in addition to you pulling by hand numerous tow bars, weighing 135 pounds each as you would eventually be hooking or attaching many of them up to a tow tractor or an aircraft so that they could be re-spotted from Fly-3 at the aft end of the flight deck to Fly-2, the midsection, or all the way up to Fly-1 at the forward section or even spotted on the elevator destined for the hanger. Consequently, after four or five cycles of that, you would be absolutely exhausted, contributing to the Blue shirt getting agitated to the point that he was not going to take any shit from anyone, including his supervisors, regardless of who he was.

At Sea:

From September 27 to October 24, 1977, both John and I, along with our fellow shipmates to include Air Wing CVW-17—which means a full complement of over five thousand sailors—sailed from Mayport, Florida, as the FID got "haze gray and underway" (a term used by sailors meaning going to sea) for refresher training, basically the preseason as I described it via an analogy previously, but this particular time we would be performing in the waters of the Caribbean. The ship became anchored off the coast of Guantanamo Bay Cuba (commonly called GITMO) over October 1–2. Then after a challenging and most demanding two weeks of being under arduous conditions constantly being graded, observed and evaluated by the Navy's Atlantic Fleet Training Group (AFTG), the ship's crew (just like a football, baseball or any sports team does after a hard fought game) looked forward to some liberty call or what some would say R& R or time off to relax in the capital city of Port-au-Prince Haiti. It was the first time either John, me and I am sure many other of the young "FID" sailors who were onboard during that time had ever been overseas as sailors on liberty, especially in Port Au-Prince, Haiti, or anywhere else from a US Navy perspective. I had such a great time that I myself got inebriated to the point that I got in trouble with the Island police up in the mountains of the Dominican Republic and eventually ended up on Class "C" liberty, which was basically a punitive action that led to me being restricted to the FID after my first day of liberty because of my maladaptive behavior. They brought me back to fleet landing in handcuffs that evening because I got in a slight altercation at a club and brothel named Copacabana. Ironically, Barry Manilow would have a hit single entitled "(At the Copa Copa) Copacabana" with lyrics that stated it was "the hottest spot north of Havana," and for years I always thought he was referring to that place. However, as time went by, I ultimately learned, many years later (when I became more of a listener) that it was inspired by his visit to the Copacabana Hotel in Rio de Janeiro.

At Sea:

John Pugioti, Fly-3 Blue shirt, work-ups January 1978

John and I, along with the ship's company and air wing got underway again on January 13, 1978, for routine workups as the FID was in full preparation for ensuring we were well trained for our upcoming Mediterranean six-month deployment. This time we were scheduled to be out for a three-week at-sea period in the Atlantic Fleet Weapons Range area, which was located just off the coast of Roosevelt Roads, Puerto Rico, which was approximately forty-nine miles off the St. Augustine, Florida, coast. As sailors we expected to be at sea, the location of where we performed our duties off the coast was not really thought about, and especially not by us Blue shirts, we were only concerned with keeping our head out of our asses, and keeping our heads on a swivel as we use to say, to ensure that we remained safe while performing at an optimum level. Training was going as usual and cycle operations were being successfully completed as per the daily air plan, but because the daily air plan called for ninety-minute cycles, the men of V-1 Division, which included Yellow shirts, Blue shirts, and others who toiled on the flight deck of the FID, were able to allow individuals to go to chow (down below decks to the mess hall to eat), which required some to go to chow and others to continue to work until they got relieved so that they in turn could go to chow afterwards while the pace of flight ops remained unfettered . In each fly, a crew would normally consist of two or three Yellow shirts with two Blue shirts assigned to each Yellow shirt.

This was because a Yellow shirt who would be the supervisor of his crew needed to be able to begin the process of taxiing (aircraft moves under its own power without aide of a tow tractor or in some situations no pushing by human beings) an aircraft by giving the appropriate hand signals to a pair of Blue shirts, who would in turn hustle underneath the aircraft and position themselves adjacent to one of the two wheel mounts (while the aircraft engine or engines depending on what type of aircraft, were running) in preparation for the Yellow shirt's next hand signal. Then immediately, without thinking critically the (Bubba as per AHO) Blue shirts would break down or unhook the tie-down chains, which were secured to the pad-eyes embedded within the steel deck of the aircraft carrier. All chains would be released including the main tie-down chains that were attached to a select area (depending on the type of aircraft) of the nose wheel and the two main mounts of that particular aircraft, as then and only then could the aircraft be staged in preparation to be taxied to another location on the carrier. In some situations, (depending on the type of aircraft or weather conditions) other reinforced areas on the aircraft were utilized with the use of additional tie-downs to ensure that the aircraft was secured to the deck to prevent it from becoming detached, however they would be removed also prior to staging. For recovery of returning aircraft, the same type of team would be required to secure an aircraft after it landed safely on the flight deck. Then it would be in reverse order, meaning a Yellow shirt would taxi the A/C over the foul line, which is a red and white line painted on the starboard side (right side) of the angled deck, stretching from the round down ramp in the Fly-3 area all the way to the end of the angled deck at the end of Fly-2 area and a few yards aft into the port side area of Fly-1. NATOPS Manuals advises that all individuals and equipment must be inboard of the foul line during A/C recovery.

On the evening of January 15, 1978, Fly-3 Blue shirts John Pugioti and I were two of four Blue shirts under the supervision of Fly-3 Petty Officer ABH2 Jesse R. Puente and Assistant Fly-3 Petty Officer ABH-3 Johnny C. Gill. On that evening, we had been flying cycle ops that particular day; John volunteered to stay on the flight deck of the FID that evening as he informed me that I should go to chow first and that he would wait for me to relieve him for chow when I returned. So some other V-1 Division flight deck crew members and I went to chow below decks in the ship's main mess deck while ABH-2 Puente, ABH-3 Gill, ABH-3 Bell, Airman John Pugioti, and several other Blue shirts, Tractor drivers, and obviously other flight deck crew members continued to re-spot aircraft on the flight deck of the FID.

After chow and almost immediately upon returning to the deck as I was coming up from the catwalk on the starboard side of the ship between the island structure and alley (an area where the E-2 Hawkeye were normally staged) so that I could relieve John for chow, a thunderous sound was heard as all of a sudden an A-7 Corsair landed suddenly without warning, striking the top of an EA6B Prowler, which was attached to a tow bar and hooked up to an aircraft tow tractor being driven by the Tractor King (ABH-3 Bell) and taxied by ABH2 Puente, being assisted by ABH-3 Gill.

All of a sudden, there was complete chaos and there were several fires of debris on the deck along with the smell of burning JP-5 fuel. Black smoke mushroomed in the air while simultaneously the emergency siren was activated. Without hesitation, the Crash and Salvage crew and others sprang into emergency mode, and before you knew it, the fires were out. Immediately, it was apparent that there were numerous casualties. I was not physically hit or struck by any debris; however, I was shocked and in disbelief initially (because we were re-spotting), and at some time I believe I was paralyzed with confusion on what to do, because as I looked to my left, I observed John Pugioti lying on his back screaming and hollering in agony, "My legs! My legs! I can't play basketball anymore!" As he was receiving medical attention, he just kept screaming as I knew he was in tremendous pain. I believed he was going in and out of shock, and in my mind, I thought he was going to die. John was eventually placed into a stokes (wire basket) stretcher which was retrieved from the flight deck emergency medical station from within the island structure and hurried off of the flight deck to a nearby aircraft elevator by what seemed like a countless number of flight deck personnel; simultaneously and in somewhat of a trance others and I began an unorganized miniature Foreign Object Debris, or "FOD," walk down, searching the flight deck, looking for other casualties, and extinguishing whatever small fires that remained from the Fly-2 area on up to the bow. We proceeded to stomp out with our feet what was perceived to be a smoldering reflash fire that was just starboard of the file line and adjacent to the six pack (area where Fly-2 would spot six F-4 Phantoms), but as we looked closer, we begain to see the outline of a green foul weather jacket, that's when we discovered that it was not debris or a reflash fire, but rather the remains of our Assist Fly-3 Petty Officer ABH-3 Johnny Gill. Immediately upon discovering this, a stokes stretcher was summoned, and his remains—as they were falling apart—were placed onto the stretcher and taken by medical personnel and others, again via aircraft elevator, to the below decks medical station. Blue shirt airman Craig Finch received lifesaving assistance from sailors on the deck that evening for the injuries he sustained as a result of his head being crushed. He was eventually taken by stretcher to the ship's medical station below decks also. Tractor King ABH-3 Bell got both of his legs crushed, as he was sitting in the driver's seat of the MD-3 tow-tractor as he towed the EA6-B when the mishap occurred. All of the dead and injured were actually in the process of re-spotting abreast the Fly–2 area, or what novice individuals would observe as the transitioning of military aircraft from the Fly-3 area to the Fly-2 area of the FID's flight deck. There was no warning at all that this would happen. Curtis Bell was also put into one of the Stokes stretchers and taken below decks to medical via an aircraft elevator. I myself observed a human esophagus that someone else retrieved as we cleaned the deck during our walk down, in addition to discovering and retrieving pieces and chunks of human flesh, which were spread about the flight deck, it continues to be difficult for me to forget even after all these years because it reminded me of large chunks of meat, similar to what I had observed from meat out of a can of Alpo dog food. We were informed that ABH2 Jesse Puente's remains were never found; however, many of us believed that the esophagus was his because the plane landed directly on top of him and took his body off of the angled deck with it. Jessie had recently gotten surgery on his big toe; it was found and identified as his remains because of the scar tissue from the earlier surgery he had prior to the aircraft mishap that took his life, I remember it like it was yesterday.

After all casualties and the deceased were discovered and taken care of, an official Foreign Object Debris i.e., FOD walk down took place, which is a normal procedure or action performed prior to any launch and recovery of aircraft. It is done to prevent foreign objects and or debris from being sucked up into aircraft engines. It was done by everyone on the deck forming a straight line at the round-down area of the Fly-3 area of the flight deck while facing forward, stretching across the flight deck from the farthest starboard side (right side facing forward) of the flight deck to the farthest port side (left side facing forward) of the flight deck. Somehow I keep thinking that we might have also initiated another one from the bow area (forward) of the flight deck also, forming a straight line, consisting of hundreds of sailors from both CVW-17 and the ship's Air Department. It would have started with each sailor walking slowly with his head down, concentrating on finding the tiniest debris that could possibly injure an individual or damage an aircraft engine, potentially leading to a malfunction that could possibly contribute to another aircraft mishap as a result of engine failure.

During this particular aircraft mishap and sometime prior to impact, the pilot ejected. What is known is that he landed safely and was treated because he had minor bruises that were taking care of after he was retrieved from the warm coastal waters of Florida. According to the Online source Naval History and Heritage Command at : // www.history.navy.mil/research/histories/ship-histories/danfs/f/for-restal-cva-59.html ., the pilot was rescued by a HS-3 Seaking search and rescue team consisting of Lt. Brian K. Young, LTJG Leland, S. Kollmorgen, AW-3 Lawrence, L. Johnson, and AW-3 Michael E. Meier, he sustained minor injuries. However, the article does not share the squardron he was with nor his military rank or name. It further states that the Sea Kings (SH-3s) flew all night, as they medically evacuated injured personnel to the NAS JAX Naval Medical Center ashore; they also continued to search the sea for other possible victims who may have been blown over the side of the *Forrestal*.

Many of us in the Air Department V-1 Division were absolutely devastated by the senseless injuries and loss of life of our friends and colleagues; in fact, and I don't know who started it, but quietly we stated to each other that because that dumb-ass pilot landed on the flight deck during re-spot, that we would not participate in flight ops the next day as a protest to what had happened so unexpectedly. Again, it made no sense to us because we were re-spotting and no landing of aircraft should have happened.

Memories from some of the injured and fallen sailors include:

ABH-2 Jessie Puente from the state of Texas was an excellent leader, authentic, and at times playful. He got the most out of the men who worked for him.

ABH-3 Johnny Gill, again born in the South possibly Kentucky, was very close to reenlisting and transferring to a new duty station; he was engaged and about to be married.

ABH-3 Curtis Bell from Chicago Illinois was one of the first petty officers I met in V-1 Division as an ABHAR, I was told by Bell during my first week on the FID, "Never turn your back on an aircraft." Bell was a short-timer with a few weeks left in the Navy; he was planning on getting out and going back home to Chicago Illinois. The ironic thing is that I never forgot about him because of what he told me, I still believe that he was joking at the time. The mishap happened when Bell had his back turned on an aircraft while performing his duties as TK, he was operating an MD-3 tow tractor and towing the EA6B Prowler that the A-7 II Corsair struck that evening.

Craig Finch, the V-1 Division Blue shirt who got his head crushed by the tire of the A-7 Corsair, survived the mishap also, and he visited the FID after he got out of the NAS JAX Naval Medical Center. It was approximately a month later when he showed up on the after brow (entrance onboard the ship for enlisted personnel) requesting someone from V-1 to escort him on the ship so that he could say thanks to some of the guys responsible for saving his life. He stated that he was going to be medically discharged from the naval service, and that was the last time we heard from him. No updates were ever given on the status of the remaining surviving sailors who were injured on the evening of January 15, 1978, on the flight deck of the USS *Forrestal CV-59*.

You are not forgotten, RIP :
ABH-2 Jesse R. Puente
ABH-3 Johnny C. Gill

Forrestal
Sailors

Off the coast of
St. Augustine, Fla.

I Was There

My Final Respot

January 15th 1978

Who was the pilot of the single-seat A7 Corsair II that ejected just prior to the Aircraft Mishap?

A salute and tribute to the men injured and killed as a result of this tragic mishap

I am sure there are others, who have never forgotten about what happened that night; how could any of us who were on the deck that evening forget . . . especially me . . . because I knew that I had just dodged a bullet, since John Pugioti elected to stay on the flight deck during that particular time and told me to go to chow first, on that fateful evening. I am blessed to have both of my legs, something that I have never forgotten. After the deck was clean of blood and debris, and when we went below on the 03 level just adjacent to the catwalk and back into the Blue shirt hole, or the Fly-3 Blue shirt locker area, I couldn't help but to look over at the locker where John Pugioti had stored his belongings. As I observed closely and reflected on what had just happened, I noticed something eerie about the entire situation that the numerous flight deck crew members and I had experienced so unexpectedly, and as I continued to look even more closely at John's locker, as I sat there staring at it and thinking that it could have been me and that he most likely (from my naive perspective) would probably not make it, I observed that John's last name was stenciled on his locker , in an eerily blood-red spray paint over spray display of large, four-inch letters. Obviously, it was done by using a can of spray paint and the standard four-inch metal stencils that we typically used to label flight deck jerseys and float coats, but because of the overspray and excessive use of spray paint, it had drippings from each letter of his last name, which appeared to me to symbolize the dripping of human blood. I made a vow to myself that evening that I would never write my name in red from that day forward and even today I still adhere to that philosophy and I shall for the remainder of my life.

4

Waking Up, Chronic and Acute Anger, Depression, Addiction, Business as Usual

Days later, John woke up and discovered his tremendous loss . . . he had no legs. He realized he was in a hospital bed at NAS JAX Naval Regional Medical Center in Jacksonville, Florida. While there, he shared a room with other sailors who were casualties of the aircraft mishap onboard the flight deck of the USS *Forrestal CV-59*. While there, the Red Cross initiated a call and made arrangements for John's parents to get to Jacksonville's Naval Hospital Regional Medical Center to comfort John while they stayed at a local military couple's residence while they were visiting their son in the hospital, at no cost to them.

Terribly frightened and stressed with thoughts that they were going to lose their only son, John, whom they loved dearly, the Pugioti couple flew as quickly as possible from New York to see their youngest child, John, as they were overwhelmed by his loss of limbs and his immediate condition. Upon arrival at the hospital and entering his room, John's parents observed him in heavy sedation, in seriously critical condition, with a plethora of serious internal injuries. Most concerning to them were his head trauma, fractured hip, and the absence of both of his lower legs.

They both continually wept openly in disbelief while expressing their love for their son; they remained in his room praying and consoling each other until John's medical condition progressed to being more stable. After this initial reaction, they realized they had questions that needed to be answered about what actually had happened to cause John's life-threatening, career-altering traumatic life scars and injuries, in addition to the death of two of his shipmates the devastating physical and psychological injuries to the other sailors, and the resulting pain and suffering to their families.

During this time, feelings of helplessness along with their deepest love for John became mixed with frustration and anger at the US Navy, because they would not provide concrete answers about the tragic incident and why it occurred. Everyone knew that a plane had crashed on the flight deck onboard the USS *Forrestal CV-59* where John and other dedicated young airmen where working—that was a given—but who was the pilot, and why did he land in a manner that caused the mishap? Specifically, they wanted to know, what was his name, and why did he land? Did he suffer major injuries himself, and if so, was he in the NAS JAX Naval Regional Medical Center in Jacksonville also? Then, too, did he have some type of aircraft malfunction, or was it pilot error? But most of all, who was the US Navy going to hold accountable for the loss of life and injuries of the individuals who became casualties as the result of someone's miscalculation, ineptness, or neglect, if that was the situation?

As they continued to press for answers, all the information that they received was that an investigation into the accident was taking place, and upon completion of a thorough investigation, a US Navy spokesman would contact the family with the results of their investigation as soon as possible. Because John's farther had to get back to work, he and his wife could not stay in the Jacksonville area very long, and eventually they were faced with making one of the most difficult decisions in their life—flying back home together to New York and leaving their beloved son John in Florida at the NAS JAX Naval Regional Medical Center in Jacksonville Florida alone.

The exact length of time John spent at NAS JAX Naval Regional Medical Center in Jacksonville, Florida, remains unknown, but one thing is for certain: when asked about it, John will tell you that he was there "long enough to hate the fucking place." According to John, who was used to being active and spending his recreational time playing sports such as basketball, football, lifting weights and running et cetera, the boredom that came with lying in his bed thinking about what happened and how it happened was driving him almost insane. He spent many days struggling to get out of his bed into a wheelchair, only to wheel his own self around a damn near empty hospital to discover nothing. In fact, on one occasion, after being there for a substantial amount of time, he and another sailor, who was also a casualty of the accident (his roommate), plotted to go to an empty floor at the hospital so that they could smoke a joint of marijuana. The memory left an indelible mark on him because it was the first time he had smoked pot without his legs, and it gave him a heightened sense of paranoia, so much so that he stopped smoking marijuana after that day.

Consequently, while in the hospital, John also became acutely depressed as reality began to sink in that he had lost his legs forever—no more basketball, which was his favorite sport, no more challenging himself to compete with others at the highest level in order to secure a sense of pride, accomplishment, and power. Challenges increased for John as a variety of emotional and psychological feelings arose in addition to the physical pain he was experiencing from his physical injuries.

Thoughts of others who were his teammates and colleagues in Air Department V-1 Division all of a sudden became visual as he envisioned various aircrafts, colored jerseys, individual faces, mannerisms, and actions of men moving aircraft, launching and recovering the FID's aircraft in perfect harmony , but without himself being there at all. Memories were overwhelming.

The daily physical and psychological pain was unbearable most of the time during the initial months or so as John's body was fighting to get acclimated to accepting not only the physical, but the emotional and psychological pain that accompanied the collective damage of such a severe traumatic experience that instantly transitioned John from being a exceptional athlete into being a double amputee.

Morphine and other strong narcotic medications were consistently pumped into John and the others who were in constant pain as a result of the mishap, on an at-will basis to ensure pain relief. Void of an appetite and with a dislike for hospital food, nurses, and others whom he believed pretended to care about him, John relished in exhibiting behavioral characteristics associated with being back home with his old crew from the Bronx. This included being pessimistic about individuals and situations where he was not with his close friends he knew from the Bronx and whom he was comfortable with. Basically, the individuals who no doubt, would typically be there for him—unlike the artificial feel of those serving him at the NAS JAX Naval Regional Medical Center in Jacksonville Florida.

According to John, he experienced nightmares and unpleasant dreams. He had numerous nights of intermittent sleep, along with sleepless and unpleasant nights. His constant review of the aircraft mishap caused intense cognitive distress. In part due to the frustration of never being given any explanations by the US Navy on what transpired on that one tragic evening, John's anguish grew more powerful; consequently, he became a more difficult person to get along with, exhibiting more obnoxious characteristics in his interactions with others. He found he enjoyed sensing the emotional pain and anguish of others as he deliberately articulated questions and answers in a manner he knew would eventually capitalize on their inability to answer, which prompted him to utilize his quick wit and a more colorful usage of language to include four-letter words; he would later explain that it was because he was a direct reflection of being a native of the Bronx, New York, and because of the situational dynamics that resulted from his active duty military experience, which had yet to be resolved or have closure.

An entire plethora of emotions overwhelmed his mind and heart at this time: loneliness, hopelessness, regret, and despair, and at intermittent intervals the thought of suicide would creep in. He battled his physiological and emotional wounds continually, the conflict exhausting his mind daily.

Consequently, the persistent feelings of severe depression and the accumulation of negativity, chronic and acute anger, hate, and rage had a ruthless effect on his thoughts, emotional state, and conduct with hospital staff. Combined with the daily infusion of medicinal drugs, John was becoming psychologically and emotionally detached from others; because his body had built a tolerance to the steady increasing stream of narcotics, he was also on his way to becoming a bona fide drug addict. Feeling isolated, discarded, discounted, and useless to others and the US Navy, he found medication to be his best friend, and all John wanted to do now was to go back home where he knew he was loved and not be pitied or patronized.

As soon as John felt stronger, on a daily basis he started calling home, asking his mother and father to do all they could to get him out of the hospital, so he could get away from the military organization that he had begun to obsessively despise. John began to harbor a deep sense of contempt and passionate hate toward that place. His hate was easily reinforced by the callous attitude of his superiors, the military systemic process, protocol, and lack of respect for an Italian American family and their nineteen-year-old active duty military service member who had volunteered for what seemed to him to do nothing but sacrifice his two legs and diminish his quality of life.

Unfortunately, there was also the fact that John was never visited by any individual from the USS *Forrestal CV-59* during his stay at the hospital in Jacksonville. There were no cards, no flowers, no phone calls, and no visitors from the FID, CVW-17 Air Wing, or any military representative on any level. The dynamics of John Pugioti's entire world began to change instantly and forever upon awakening and discovering he had lost his legs, and it appeared that nobody from the United States Navy or any other government entity gave a damn.

Eventually, John's persistent and constant calling of his parents to get him transferred to a VA hospital close to his home and loved ones, coupled with the unconditional love Mr. and Mrs. Pugioti had for their son, all culminated into a powerful movement of shared frustration and disappointment that the US Navy and the military service could no longer ignore. Then, finally, with the assistance of a politically connected neighbor in New York, the Pugioti family accomplished the results they wanted. The key influential person, as described by John, was an older lady who resided across from the Pugioti residence in the Bronx, New York. As a result of their conversations with her, she successfully used her influence in a manner that eventually played an integral part in the Pugioti family getting their loved one transferred to the Bronx VA Hospital, on Kingsbridge Avenue in New York.

In preparation to be transferred via military medical evacuation, John was strapped down on a mobile stretcher by US Navy corpsmen, which he stated admittedly "freaked him out"; it was done in that manner to ensure that he remained secure during his flight on a C-9 military medical transport plane flown from the NAS JAX Naval Regional Medical Center in Jacksonville, to a local New York airport and then taken via ambulance to the James J. Peters VA Medical Center, located at 130 West Kingsbridge Road, Bronx, New York. One could only imagine the intense anxiety that John must have experienced even thinking about an airplane in regards to taxiing, landing, taking off, and flying, especially after the trauma that he had already been through as a result of his final re-spot, which ultimately ended in him becoming a casualty as a result of the aircraft mishap on the USS *Forrestal CV-59*.

Back on the FID, after the mishap on January 15, it was business as usual for CVW-17, Air Department, V-1 Division andall others who worked on the flight deck of the USS Forrestal CV-59. The FID participated in several other underway periods in continued preparation for its Mediterranean cruise, which began on April 4 and ended when the FID returned home to Mayport, Florida, on October 26, 1978.

By the conclusion of the six-month deployment, I was promoted and became ABH-3 Etheridge, hence I went from being primarily just one of the physical laborers or one of the Bubba's, to working inside the air-conditioned confines of flight deck control along with the Aircraft Handler and other decision makers. Yes, I was excited that I no longer had to physically move aircraft on the flight deck or carry chalks and chains, because now I was being given a ticket to become branded as being more cerebral (which is what I was more comfortable with) and I was delighted for the opportunity to move templates of CVW-17 aircraft on the Ouija board, which was a mathematically scaled-down version of the actual flight and hanger decks of the USS *Forrestal CV-59.*

After the 1978 Mediterranean deployment and a short stint in the Naval Station Mayport Shipyard for routine maintenance and repairs, the FID began its workups again, but by September 1979, I had received new orders to Misawa Air Base, Japan. Other national events that were parallel to the Navy events in 1979 included: in the sports world the nation observed the Seattle Supersonics defeat the Washington Bullets in the National Basketball Association Finals, and the Major League Baseball's World Series was captured by the Pittsburgh Pirates, while in the National Football League, the Pittsburgh Steelers defeated "America's team," the Dallas Cowboys, for bragging rights to the Vince Lombardi Trophy. In music, folks were enjoying the sounds of Pink Floyd's *The Wall*, Donna Summers's "Hot Stuff" and "Bad Girls," in addition to the Bee Gees' "Love You Inside Out."

While I was stationed at Misawa Air Base, Japan, unbelievably it happened again. A United States Navy Aircraft Carrier had an aircraft mishap on its flight deck. In May of 1981, the USS *Nimitz CVN-68* was struck by tragedy on the flight deck. It happened during work-ups while off the coast of Florida, but this time it was an EA6-B that crashed on the starboard side of the flight deck of CVN-68. There were multiple losses of life and dozens of casualties, including Air Department (ABHs), Air Wing personnel and other company person-nel. Again, casualties were sent to NAS JAX Naval Regional Medical Center in Jacksonville, just like with John and the other casualties from the tragedy on the FID on January 15, 1978.

5

The Son of Sam Law

For over seventy-five years, the James J. Peters VA Medical Center, located at 130 West Kingsbridge Road, Bronx, New York, has provided medical services to all US military veterans. Even to this day, it is the oldest veteran's affairs (VA) facility in New York City and the second largest VA facility in the nation.

In 1979, upon John's arrival at the old hospital, which preceded the current James J. Peters VA Medical Center which was built in1981, it had some serious challenges. In fact, during that era nationwide, all VA hospitals were facing budget cuts and financial difficulties with the ending of the Vietnam Conflict, i.e., war. Politically, citizen unrest and antiwar protests had somewhat cooled down, but the toxicity within the environment as a result of the Vietnam war had soured the nation on most anything associated with the military, especially spending.

Consequently, as it has been widely written in periodicals and bulletins like the one written by Kitty Bennett for AARP on December 20, 2011, about Ron Kovic, the subject of the movie *Born on the Fourth of July*, it was because of the lack of federal funding that the quality of life for veterans admitted to James J. Peters VA Medical Center in the Bronx as well as many other older VA medical facilities during that particular era was deplorable and disgraceful. That said, John shared his thoughts with me as he spoke candidly about the time he spent there at the James J. Peters VA Medical Center in 1978; and according to John, there was no question that there were some serious challenges during that particular era there. Hence, he urged me to review Born on the Fourth of July, a movie featuring Tom Cruise, that shares the real-life challenges of Ron Kovic via his story of being a paralyzed Vietnam-era veteran who basically shared with the nation and the entire world what John observed doing that era of time regarding the level of care and sanitation at the James J. Peters VA Medical Center Bronx New York. With politicians lack of government funding and a distain for the war and military veterans during the end of the Vietnam war, it's rather easy to understand why rooms were not well kept and the lack of basic housecleaning services resulted in individuals routinely seeing pests like cockroaches intermittently during the day, evening, and night scavenging on unwanted food, human stool or feces, and urine in various locations.

Eventually the pests problem and its neglected and dilapidated structures—i.e., hallways, doors, windows, and rooms—contributed to its eventual demise and subsequent replacement by the outstanding facility that it is today, which is no comparison to the foul odor from mildew and rodent droppings from mice and large rats of a shameful era from the past. In fact, when John and I met for the first time in September 2015 at the new James J. Peters VA Medical Center, I was so impressed with the treatment of my arrival and assistance by the staff when I requested a place to meet with John (so that we could talk for the first time face to face since that horrible evening of January 15, 1978) that I wrote an article on LinkedIn Pulse about it, the tight security presence, and the eagerness of the staff and management to accommodate a meeting space for John and me. It was a far cry from what I could have assumed from my experience as an advocate for veterans, as I myself have encountered situations in which I believe that overworked and ineptly trained staff only wanted to ensure that they kept their job security, so they underreported things and situations that might negatively affect veterans, their families or loved ones, for I am sure there are a variety of reasons.

To give a better perspective of the times being that John was there in the late '70s and early '80s , which was an era in which one could easily imagine patients recreationally smoking pot in any VA Medical Center and even in some situations veterans who were staff members and others could easily smuggle in paraphernalia to smoke marijuana themselves or with the very clients that were there, and it was most likely because of a lack of funding to hire individuals to monitor what probably was obviously happening during that era.

However, regardless of the unsanitary situation regarding the James J. Peters VA Medical Center Bronx New York at that time, which was again a direct reflection of government cut-backs, John exhibited the strength to persevere. The bottom line was this: the lack of sanitary conditions did not matter as much to John as being back in his beloved hometown where he knew he was close to people whom he loved, and they loved him, in the Bronx, New York.

Still, there were no answers from the US Navy or anyone from the military on what happened the evening of January 15, 1978; then, on March 15, exactly two months after the mishap, the United States Navy discharged John by placing him on their permanent disability retirement list. They expedited separating him from the military service, but for some unknown reason, information about the event was never given. The night of the aircraft mishap on the USS *Forrestal CV-59* remained a foggy nightmare and mystery especially for him but also his family members too.

John's rehabilitation at the VA hospital was extremely painful, so they started immediately with the continuation of pain medications consisting of a variety of narcotics along with physical exercises for rehabilitation of the residual limbs that now exist where there used to be John's legs. To say or hear the words "stumps" at that time, as the hospital staff—including physicians—would call them then during that era, it only enhanced his anger and reminded him of how much he regretted joining the military, especially the Navy. It got to the point that his primary mindset revealed characteristics associated with being passive-aggressive as he rebelled at the sound of their voices out of pure anger for his unenviable situation; added to that was the fact that he was fighting internally about surrendering to the realization that someone had to teach or assist him with helping himself as if he was a insecure individual or a child.

John's physical therapy and rehabilitation treatment was designed to get him to feel comfortable moving his limbs around after such a catastrophic and traumatic life-altering experience. Every day there was a series of physical exercises that the physical therapist assisted him with; there was a specific type and method of exercise for his residual limb below the knee with his right limb and another for his injury above the knee on his left limb.

Exercises for the below-the-knee injury were specifically designed for keeping the hip and knee free by his placing a couple of pillows on the bed while sitting up and placing the residual limb on the pillow enough so it hung over the pillows and then starting, working the muscle and the residual limb in its entirety up and down as if lifting the leg up and down continuously. Painful and grueling (especially where the stitches and the scar tissue were), at times it felt as if the muscles were tearing from one another or the bone; he would begin sitting on the edge of the bed with both hands supporting and balancing the body and doing the same thing, lifting the residual limb up and down, supposedly always slowly to gain maximum pain. "No pain, no gain," they would say.

For the residual limb above the knee (left limb), it was done initially with the assistance of the physical therapist. The starting position would be lying on the body's right side while on the bed, with the initial session being led by a physical therapist who assisted with moving the residual limb in various directions, causing the most unbearable and excruciating pain ever. During the first session in particular, at one point, prior to moving his residual limb forward, back up and down, the therapist accidently placed her hand on some scar tissue, prompting immediate discomfort, and an intense pain seared through his body, forcing John to shout out repeatedly and rapidly at a cacophonous level, several rounds of rapid-fire expletives which she would never forget.

After that initial demonstration of new and more advanced exercise, he knew it was just the beginning of what would turn out to be a long rehab and fight to walk on his own again. John continued to receive assistance along with monitoring and was informed to follow his scheduled rehabilitation routine. If there was any discomfort or pain, he was to ask for pain control medication as he felt he needed them.

Assigned to the amputee ward of the hospital, John was one of (if not *the*) youngest veterans there; most of the veteran amputees were combat Vietnam or Korean War–era veterans who themselves were lonely, bitter, angry, and disappointed with the way the country expressed a lack of gratitude for the sacrifice they had made for their country. This was especially true for the Vietnam veterans as they came home to ridicule (they were dubbed as baby killers, war mongers, drug addicts, etc.) from many American citizens who opposed the war. They had become political pawns in a situation where Congress did not officially declare Vietnam as a war; therefore, some called it merely a conflict.

As a result of the controversy, along with the advancement of technology (television) and the daily viewing of news reported by the iconic anchor Walter Cronkite and celebrity anchors such as Roger Mud, Dan Rather, Tom Brokaw, and others (via black-and-white television), American citizens got a bird's-eye view and observation of the ugliness of war—right there at home in their own living rooms at their dinner tables. Consequently, their journalistic views (the reporter's of that era) had a profound effect on the perception and reality of the nation's viewers, and it contributed to American's distaste for Vietnam and all that it stood for.

Even the great state of Virginia, with the state's economy depending on military spending and jobs, with the Norfolk Naval Shipyard

(Navy Town USA), which was the former home port of the FID prior to it relocating to Mayport (North Florida, South Georgia) in the Jacksonville, Florida, area, was not immune to the toxicity associated with the negativity toward Vietnam-era military personnel, because during those times (the '70s) it was not uncommon to see signs posted in folks' yards stating, "No Dogs or Sailors on the Grass" in the Norfolk, Virginia, area. One could only imagine how confusing and unappreciated that could make a young nineteen- or twenty-something year old feel, especially when they were stationed hundreds of miles from their hometown and were greeted with such hypocrisy. As a result, many veterans of the Vietnam era responded in a typical, yet predictable manner, based upon mistreatment and the disappointment received from others. For many of them, their behaviors included acting out with anger and rage, along with self-medicating to mask the emotional and psychological pain and trauma they had experienced or observed and subject to after returning home. They heavily indulged in the use of marijuana, hallucinogens, heroin, or any other illicit drugs that they could take by any means necessary. Unbeknownst to many, they simply compounded their situation—actually enhancing their probability of becoming addicted, for as an amputee, in too many cases they were prescribed immoral amounts of morphine as a staple for pain management, and unfortunately it is trending in a similar direction in today's society.

Being so young, uninformed on what had happened to him, and unfamiliar with the policies and procedures of the military, John could only rely on the answers and behaviors that he obtained from his fellow amputees in his hospital ward who were bitter and angry themselves with the government and also their own situational dynamics. With that said, he also had something many of them did not have—the fact that his family lived less than thirty minutes away from him. Because his family lived in close proximity to the hospital, John's mother faithfully brought him dinner every evening, on the weekend he would go home and spend time with friends and family members.

It was party time every weekend for John and the regular crew; others would come over, bring food and adult beverages; they would get high on a variety of substances and have a blast with him as they all wanted him to feel as if things were normal, and it was their way of sharing their love and respect for him. Eventually John, being the strong-willed individual that he was, grew tired and fed up with being an amputee patient in the VA hospital; the occupational therapist and others had given him what he felt was a new lease on his life, so he packed his things, grabbed his stuff, and literally walked out on his own, never to return in that capacity or under those circumstances. It was his way of showing his autonomy, perseverance, and determination to do things as he had done them in the past.

The beautiful classic 1981 Oldsmobile Tornado

It took almost two years before John's claim for service-connected disability came through. Ahh, but when it came, it was all in a lump sum! The first thing that he did was purchase a second-generation, brand-new, metallic-blue 1981 Oldsmobile Tornado two-door coup with a 252 cu in (4.13l) V6 with all the bells and whistles. It was an absolutely beautiful vehicle during its time and a classic for individuals to showcase today. For John, it exemplified everything he stood for, which was excellence, and it garnered the respect and dignity that he felt and knew he did not get as a result of sacrificing his limbs on the flight deck of the USS *Forrestal CV-59*. John's family and friends were so happy for him; they loved the fact that he was finally getting what he rightfully deserved, in addition to seeing progress, and it seemed as if things were coming together for him as he prepared to move forward in his new life as a service-connected disabled veteran and double amputee.

By this time also, John's use of prescribed medication (morphine and other narcotics) from the military medical center, his constant self-medicating, and partying had led him to become an addict and helped to keep him in denial regarding his substance abuse and addiction. His paranoia, anxiety, and shortness with people and situations that he was not fond of could easily be comparable to characteristics associated with withdrawals of an alcoholic or cocaine or heroin addict. John's reality became so distorted that his entire persona was attached to a perception of who and what he was; this also included his vehicle, so much so that one day while driving his vehicle in the Bronx, and after stopping at a convenience store to get some gas, he was confronted with unfounded accusations against him by two individuals, and one thing led to another. As a result of transactions during this encounter, John's beautiful, recently washed and waxed 1981 metallic-blue Oldsmobile Tornado was hit by another vehicle.

Then, unfortunately, shots were fired, and as a result, two victims were seriously wounded, and John was positively identified as the shooter. As a result of the incident, John was subsequently convicted and was sentenced up state to Green Haven Correctional Facility to serve six to eighteen years. Eventually, he was transferred after five years and sent to a lower-level medium facility with dormitories. He hated it because, as he stated, "It was soft." But because of his acute rage and perpetual chronic anger, another violent assault occurred, which resulted in him being transferred back to Green Haven but this time on a federal bid, which led to John serving time at Rikers Island.

During that era and also starting back in the summer of 1976, (nearly two years or more before our mishap on the FID) a serial killer and former US Army service member named David Berkowitz used a .44 caliber hand gun to seriously injure and kill multiple people, cowardly and cold-bloodedly attacking unsuspecting couples or individuals randomly thought New York City. That summer was a terrifying one for many New Yorkers, and it still evokes conversations about the results of his case in today's society. When he finally was captured by the police on August 10, 1977, during questioning, according to information about him on biography.com, Berkowitz explained that he had been commanded to kill by his neighbor Sam Carr, who sent messages to him through Carr's dog.

Months were spent facilitating psychological evaluations on Berkowitz to determine if he was fit to stand trial. He was eventually found fit, and in August of 1978 Berkowitz pleaded guilty to six killings and later received twenty-five years to life for each murder. The Berkowitz case is important because it could be problematic to a degree that it prohibits the authors of this book to provide any further information about the situation that caused John to be incarcerated for years in New York State Federal Prison. Also, according to Wikipedia, the law simply states that it is an American law designed to keep criminals from profiting from the publicity of their crimes by selling their story to publishers. Again, it is because of the possibility of violating such law, which is now applied as the law in forty-eight American states that we shall adhere to it. [6]

Therefore, the actual details of John's crime shall not be discussed any further. During that time, as John was serving and paying his debt to society, as a result of his maladaptive behaviors, which were fuel by his chronic and acute anger, coupled with his addiction to

6   Wikipedia contributors, "Son of Sam law," *Wikipedia, The Free Encyclopedia,* http://en.wikipedia.org/w/index.php?title=Son_of_Sam_law&oldid=660863163 (accessed May 21, 2015).

alcohol and other substances, some of the eyewitness who were present during John's injuries in V-1 Division in 1978, including me, returned to the FID for another tour and successfully completed the 1982 Mediterranean cruise onboard USS *Forrestal CV-59*. However, shortly after returning to Mayport from that deployment, the FID loaded up the Flight and Hanger Deck again with personal vehicles like it did when she relocated from its original Norfolk Home Port to change home port to Mayport, except this time it was for a major maintenance overhaul in the Philadelphia Pennsylvania shipyard for a twenty-eight-month maintenance rehabilitation called Service Life Extension Program, or SLEP.

During that 1982 Mediterranean deployment also, I was promoted again and received orders to serve a short term (two years) on USS *Saratoga CV-60* prior to being transferred to Naval Air Station Jacksonville Florida and performing the duties of a military police officer.

6

Changing the Dynamics

Following the invasion of Kuwait on August 2, 1990 Desert Shield began as the United States and the UK sent troops to Kuwait; during this time also the United States entered a major recession, which eventually had serious repercussions worldwide. *The Simpsons* was seen for the first time on Fox TV, the Berlin Wall fell, and East and West Germany reunited.

Education on any level is a key to perpetual success; knowledge is power

Meanwhile, in prison, John earned an associate's degree and was eventually released from prison in early 1990. Shortly after his return to mainstream society, he and his soon-to-be wife had their daughter, on August 13, 1990, but by late September during the same year, John had become an ardent recidivist, rotating in and out of incarceration a couple of times until he finally got tired of it, and remained out for good in1992.

With maturity and stability, he and his fiancée decided to get married, and John challenged himself as he became a responsible husband, farther, and stepdad (as his wife had a son who was three years older than their daughter), a stark difference from continuing to exhibit recklessness, chronic and acute anger to all who crossed his path.

With John's newfound love and family, the Pugioti couple saved their money together and eventually purchased a home in Rockland County New York, and they remained as a family, according to John, for as many as six or seven years, but it eventually ended. Unfortunately, it did, just like almost 50 percent or more of the married population in the nation, their marriage also ended in divorce.

After John lost his family, the change in the dynamics had a profound effect on John's attitude and demeanor, and it eventually lead John to relocate back to his roots as he fell in love all over again, but this time it was not with a woman. It was with his first love: the streets of the Bronx, New York. Being back, John would say was nothing to brag about, but it was what he felt comfortable with, and the burden of paying child support was no joke financially as it was a serious drain on his social lifestyle.

In an attempt to fill the void of his marriage being dissolved, John morphed his character and picked up with a sport he had always loved and at which he was exceptionally good, the sport of basketball.

Before the mishap, John was a prolific basketball player. He is number twenty-three

During those times, wheelchair basketball was, and it still is, quite a big thing. A lot of the NBA teams sponsored wheelchairs teams with their names, and John earned a spot on the wheelchair basketball team called the New Jersey Nets, an NBA team, who have since changed ownership and their name to the Brooklyn Nets.

The team traveled all over the United States of America to play wheelchair basketball. John's dad would be there; he absolutely loved it, especially since he was there with John and the team to see every game. That said, even though he had to pay extra for his dad's hotel room, it was well worth it to John because his father was his rock and his pillar of strength when he needed him; he was always there for him. Again, as stated earlier, John was pretty good at the game of basketball, as is evidenced by him making the all-star team every season. However, it wasn't as easy as it looked; it was a grind physically and mentally, and after numerous years with nagging injuries, John got tired and eventually retired his jump shot, his basketball wheelchair, and his sneakers.

During this time also he was going to school and riding his beloved Harley Davidson motorcycle with his friends from some select motorcycle clubs.

The motorcycle clubs were not your ordinary neighborhood clubs. They were referred to as let's just say (for privacy reasons) that most of them were not your "Little Boys Clubs" because they did not play on the mainstream side of the street, some of them from the Bronx, Brooklyn, and Queens, associated with the New York City Hells Angels, and even though he was on state and federal parole during that time, he was and remains even to this day amazed that he never violated again. That said, as John would candidly tell you, being an ex-offender and designated two-time loser (he was neither a rat nor a rapist) was a great experience for John. But he began doing things that started moving him away from that type of lifestyle, and little did he know that his life was about to change for the better, forever.

John during his Motor Cycle Club days

Yes, he recruited, i.e., prospected, for Motorcycle club members during the day, the evenings, and even during the wee hours in the morning, but unbeknownst to most, John was also an aspiring student at Lehman College, working on his bachelor's degree, which he earned in psychology.

Shortly after obtaining his bachelor's degree, his VA vocational counselor suggested he stay in school to earn his graduate degree, and two years later while attending Hunter College, he earned his graduate degree in education.

Educated and motivated, John eventually became a trained vocational educational counselor. He would have stayed in school to earn a doctorate, but according to him, the VA has been somewhat uncooperative with him and others when it comes to assisting individuals with earning their doctorate.

He shared with me how it was explained to him: "the VA does not like to fund Doctorates because they are too open ended," meaning no one knows how long it will take to complete. Also, as stated by John, "It's kind of idiotic seeing as how far they have helped me with my education."

As for veterans and anyone else for that matter, the importance of education can never be undervalued. Education opens doors when or where there are no doors, creates hope when there is no hope or where there is disenfranchisement, and opens minds when critical thinking is viewed as soft, weak, disloyal, and obsolete.

After successfully completing practicum studies with the Vocational and Educational Services for Individuals with Disabilities, which is also known as VESID, John was hired as a VESID counselor. John's practicum performance went flawless, with the exception that he began it during the week of the September 11, 2001, when the United States of America was hit by multiple coordinated terrorist attacks.

John, being a hard charger by design, became passionate about his job as a counselor, but unfortunately, he would have to resign from his position because of governmental ineffectiveness, in regards to bureaucracy.

He found out that because he had secured viable and sustained full-time employment, that within a twelve-month time span he would no longer be eligible to receive Social Security benefits. Never one to give up, he attempted to work again later at a huge auto auction in Newburg, New York. But once again the problem with losing his Social Security benefits made him make the decision to deal with reality, so he walked away from it, and he has never attempted to work again.

The balance of nature has its own way of evening the score for all of us, as we push harder and go faster without taking time out to adhere to being autonomous individuals; the very nature from which we were delivered shall call for our return.

That said, as shared by John, the best analogy one can describe regarding the biker world of which he has been enamored with is the depiction exhibited on the TV series known as the *Sons of Anarchy*. The show is or was as real as the world John was living in, which included drugs and fighting on a regular basis, and although John would state that he did not have any fights, he would also say that it was only because of him being a double amputee, which would not make him a very good fighter.

During that time also, John began taking Tai Kwon Do classes. But later he would realize that it came with a social liability, because it facilitated a mentality to think and behave in a manner as though he had a chip on his shoulder. Again, according to John, he was basically thinking that he was more invincible than the he really was.

The very nature of his associates during those times dictated that he stay out partying and riding for days. One day, while riding into a weekend without sleep and just drinking and drugging, John crashed his bike and ended up with a traumatic brain injury, or TBI.

As a result, John was on life support for over a month. But prior to the incident happening, he had already become the vice president of one of the motorcycle clubs he was a member of, and because he was unable to perform his duties for the club, he was stripped of his position.

John was greatly disappointed again because of it, and it took him a little over one year to actually get back to living with some sense of normalcy again after his biker years. Determined as ever, John eventually weaned himself off of all the medication he was on, which was an enormous amount and what some may consider an insurmountable task, but like always, John preserved. Prior to that decision and ultimate transformation, he exhibited characteristics associated with various levels of depression and would take, at a minimum, at least seven or more different pills a day and sleep a lot. But again he eventually got off all the medication and started living a full "drug free" life again. Discovering oneself is the key to bettering oneself, and now with his life back on track, John began a relationship with a new girlfriend; over time she eventually moved in with him, and according to him, she was a great help for him at that time or that season in his life.

Their romance got to the point that she wanted to marry him, but she had already been married three times prior, according to John. So he made a promise to himself that he would not be her fourth husband. Later, he found out that he was actually right about that situation because she did get married a fourth time, which again ended in divorce. Yes, life goes on, and there is no doubt that it is cyclical.

John now lives in upstate New York, of which he states, most of the time, it is an uneventful place to reside, especially if you are seeking exciting times as a hellraiser. According to John, the biggest events they usually have are when it snows for a couple of days straight and they get it by the foot, which he states is not very pleasant. As shared with me, he says he is saving to be able to buy a foreclosed house in

Florida, so he can get away from the winter, basically become a snow bird. All in all, John expresses life as a double amputee as one that really does SUCK big time, but the other alternative of being six feet under doesn't appeal to him, not one bit; he would much rather be bored watching the snow in the middle of winter.

However, John does wish that they had today's sophisticated prosthetics when this whole thing happened to him. He stated, "Who knows—I might have tried to reenlist or something," but for sure he wants to go back to school to get his doctorate degree.

7

Thank You, Shipmate

We must remember that there are infinite differences between men and all other creatures on God's earth, each with its own originality and uniqueness. As for humanity, each person's story begins Innocently authentic and morphs into something dynamic beyond one's imagination.

None of us are privy to writing our own life's script in advance of who we become; however, too many times we draw conclusions from what we hear, have experienced or observed. We assume that manmade objects, which were designed to withstand the ferocity of nature's winds, the harmful rays emitted from the sun, or even the ocean's strongest and tallest waves, would remain intact or afloat no matter how deep the channel or how far blue-water ops takes a man-made war vessel over the most turbulent seas.

But when all our scientifically designed efforts fail, we have no answers; we cover things up, or we look for others to blame. No one can ever predict with 100 percent accuracy that things will work as planned, because to be human is to be fallible. The inevitability of such a tragic mishap on the evening of January 15, 1978 can never be erased from the memories of those who were there, for it has left an indelible mark on the casualties and the families of the deceased victims of that infamous tragic day, and it has also left question marks for their loved ones, shipmates, friends, the United States Navy, and the legacy of the greatest warship built and launched on December 11, 1954 by Newport News Shipbuilding and Dry Dock Co., Newport News, Virginia.

Where are the answers to what really happened on that evening? Who was the pilot of the A-7 Corsair II that crashed onto the flight deck, killing two flight deck crew members assigned to V-1 Division and injuring others, ultimately changing the dynamics of what should have been a normal routine re-spot into a tragedy for so many? On the FID during that moment in time, scuttlebutt, i.e., speculation by sailors who were there, led many who were there, including me, to believe that it was the Executive Officer of ATKRON 81 (Attack Squadron) who was one of the assigned squadrons of CVW-17 and stationed onboard the carrier at that time.

Speculation is all we have after almost forty years with no real transparency. Also, why is there so very little published information on this tragedy, and even when there is some information discovered, the name of the pilot never gets revealed. It's the taproot of why John continues to have intermittent thoughts initiated and influenced by chronic and acute anger at himself and others in general, because in his mind, he has never been respected enough to get an answer to the question that is most important to him since the tender, naive age .of eighteen.

Talking about leadership, what were the reasons behind not telling John and his family, along with the other families who lost loved ones and careers, and let us not forget every individual (it was just not John) who in essence became eternally traumatized victims maimed or disfigured for life emotionally, physically, and psychologically? It is utterly both ridiculous and senseless that here we are over thirty-seven years later, and we still don't know what really happened or what contributed to the mishap then or now. No phone calls, no apologies, no visits from any of the leadership from the world's most influential controller and protector of the sea lanes, the absolute leader regarding military sea power, the United States Navy. So, was or is it a cover-up? Because John and I, as well as others who were there, certainly believe so, that is why this book was written. The story had to be restarted, the discussion rekindled. It takes someone or some individuals with innate talents that transcends status quo thinking, individuals who are not afraid to light an authentic fire that initiates a new investigation into discovering the facts, with an honest and a transparent intent on finding out what really happened that evening. Was it simply human error or an act of nature that caused this little known and spoken about US Navy Aviation mishap, which should have never occurred while flight deck crewmembers were re-spotting aircraft in preparation for their next launch and recovery, as they sailed approximately fifty miles off of the coast of St. Augustine, Florida, on the evening of January 15, 1978.

A young man and his shipmates encountered the dynamics of a situation that altered their minds via physical and psychological trauma, death and destruction, but by the grace of God and the resiliency of the human spirit, they moved forward and prospered, each taking their own path. Yet the leadership of the very entity that was responsible for creating opportunities for John, his shipmates, and the nation's success or failure from a global perspective left John, the families of all the victims, and his shipmates with no answers on what went wrong and how it led to such a tragic evening. They say that time has a way of healing things, but to individuals who have been traumatized, without having an understanding of why, then time only masks the pain because it's just a Band-Aid on that particular situation.

The power of the human spirit is something that you can't see nor touch. It goes beyond simple logic; it's spiritual, a component of nature. Even though it's been almost forty years since the second most devastating aircraft mishap on the flight deck of the USS *Forrestal* *CV-59* , those who were there realize that it could have been worse. With the worst being the aircraft mishap and subsequent huge historic conflagration that cost the lives of 134 sailors while the FID was on Yankee station in the Gulf of Tonkin, on July 29, 1967, it's what the public no doubt remembers. Compared to that most talked about, televised and re-evaluated (for training purposes) tragedy, the mishap that we were a part of could seem minor in the eyes of others. However, regardless of what critiques might say, the bottom line is that intuitively those who were there on Sunday evening January 15, 1978 have never forgotten, and we shall take it to our graves just like the FID sailors in the Gulf of Tonkin in 1967. During my research, I had an opportunity to locate the whereabouts of some of our ship-mates who were there on the flight deck of the USS *Forrestal CV-59* on the evening of January 15, 1978, and here is what these eyewit-nesses and traumatized victims themselves had to say. I have written each account of what they observed based upon what they sent to me via their own written statement that they either sent to me via email or snail mail.

From Air Department V-1 Division Airman Jessie Lopez (Fly–2 Blue shirt) and eyewitness who was on the flight deck that evening during the mishap:

> *We were re-spotting aircraft at night, I was a fly 2 blue shirt, I was in the landing area when I noticed a jet that looked like it was getting ready to land but since we were re-spotting I figured they would get close then fly off like always but no, this one looked like it was getting too low it looked like it was gonna land, the landing area was full of people moving air-craft I started running, and took a few steps then I saw the jet strike the top of the jet being moved.*

> *There was an explosion then the jet skidded off the flight deck. I ran behind the island then started back to see if I could help in any way, the jet that was struck caught fire but it was put out quickly. I went looking around and I seen a body lying on the flight deck, but I knew there was nothing I could do for him. Close to the body I seen a boot, the sole was cut away and could see the toes in the boot.*

---

*I then started to look for my close friend Airmen Craig Finch,
who was off to the side of the crash but he had gotten hit in
the head by the tire of the jet when it exploded and he was
already on a stretcher. I then rode down the elevator with my
friend Craig Finch and some of the other casualties. When we
got down to the hanger bay, there is where I saw John Pugioti,
he was screaming " get them off my legs their hurting my legs "
then I looked closer and I saw that his legs were in a stretcher
next to him. I will never forget this. This was the worst tragedy
I have ever been involved in. I saw shattered ankles, broken
legs, numerous injuries, I remember John Pugioti as a stand up
guy the kind of guy that took no shit off of anybody. I remember him jumping on S.O. during the morning roll call my fellow shipmate and friend Craig Finch was in the Navy around
1 year 6 months when this accident happened. He eventually
got a 100% disability check in the mail every month for the
remainder of his life. I hope this will help John get whatever
assistance or compensation he deserves.*

Jesse Lopez Airman E-3 V1 Division active 8-29-76 thru 8-29-80

From Air Department V-1 Division Airmen Jeffery A. West (Elevator #
2 Operator on the day and time of the mishap):

*I was an Elevator Operator for V-1 Division at the time. I had
been moving planes and helicopters up and down elevator
number Two, which was just aft of the Island structure.*

*While we were in the middle of "re-spotting" (moving) the
aircraft around getting set up for the next launch. I saw John
Pugeti (a blue shirt) walking beside the aircraft while "Bell"
the tractor operator was maneuvering the aircraft under Jesse
Puentes directions. Meanwhile Johnny Gill (the Fly 3 Assistant*

Director) was waiting further down the flight deck getting ready for Jesse to pass the aircraft off to him. It was then, that I began to hear a sound in the distance; it was the sound of an incoming aircraft, during the middle of us performing our duties during a routine re-spot. One in which was not suppose to be there. I looked around the deck to see if there was anything that would indicate to me that an aircraft was suppose to land, but then all of a sudden it seemed as if out of know where I saw an A-7 aircraft coming in for a flight deck landing and I was almost paralyzing shocked. I thought to myself, why is this aircraft attempting a landing while we are re-spotting?

I could not believe my eyes what was happening; it was like in slow motion an A-7 is about to crash on top of all of my shipmates. I saw the Yellow Shirt Assistant Fly-3 Director (Johnny Gill) disappear into the intake of that A-7. He was killed instantly. After which, I observed body parts laying everywhere. It was a total hellish nightmare, I observed men running everywhere grabbing hoses and stretchers. I also witnessed the canopy of the aircraft open and the pilot ejecting out of the plane. I can't recall what ever happened to the pilot. I recall telling the hanger deck operator what was happening and to leave the elevator in the up position on the flight deck so that I could send him down the casualties as they were soon to come.

I then hurriedly exited my position in the cat walk and assisted other shipmates as we picked up body parts and placed them next to stretchers which were being placed onto (elevator number two) my assigned elevator. Upon completion, I remanded the elevator two operators position in the starboard cat walk, then I put back on my head phones and informed the hanger deck control Ouija Board operator that we were ready to move the casualties down into the hanger level, so that they could be transported to the Forrestal's sick bay area.

As I remained at my post, I observed the crash and salvage crew members and others push aircraft, tractors and equipment off the deck into the sea like they were leftovers into a giant garbage disposal. Then I observed a group of the Ships Company and Air Wing Seventeen crew members begin to wash all the blood and debris off the flight deck itself.

I then heard over the ship's PA system "Let's Get Ready for Flight Deck Operations" like nothing happened. I could not believe it. I was devastated, dazed and in shock of what just went down. I went into flight deck control to see what was going on and heard over the Five MC speaker system from the Air Boss make a statement "that people on the flight deck come a dime a dozen". To this day, it continues to make me feel like we were all just trash on a giant steel receptacle. The event was one of the most tragic events in my life. I will always mourn and cherish those moments that I had with my injured and killed shipmates from V-1 Division, I still have found memories of ABH-3 Johnny Gill, who was a great team member and ABH-2 Jessie Puente who was like a big brother to all of us. For me, I witnessed something that was so tragic that others would like to have forgotten, but the memories have and probably will continue to always haunt me. I would also like to say that I am sorry I lost touch with you all, but it is sometimes easier to block the pain and grief in unspoken words. I will never forget that day, for the remainder of my life.

ABH-1 Jeffery A. West USN (Ret.) Service Connected Disabled Veteran.

From CVW-17 Squadron VS-30, Airmen Paul L. Cobb Plan Captain, eyewitness who was on the flight Deck that evening during the mishap:

This is a night I have not forgotten and memories still haunt a young man of 19 years of age. Our carrier thought all planes were onboard and all was safe, but 1 plane remained out there in the night, while the men of our ship respotted aircraft and with men moving about the aft flight deck. The pilot of that lone plane from squadron VA-81 got the ok to land on the flight deck with men and aircraft in harm's way. By the time he sees it was a fouled deck, it was too late to pull up, he had to eject into the waters and his plane crashed through the flight deck killing Jonny Gill from Kentucky and Jessie Puente from Texas and 10 other injured, so they say. I was a Brown shirt for VS-30 squadron and fortunately I came on the flight deck and first thing I see is a man in a pilot uniform on fire and a medic wearing work gloves trying to put him out with his hands. I stood in bewilderment and shock for at least a couple of minutes and felt a sickness inside my stomach and was so scared so I left the flight deck and went below where our work quarters were. It was very quiet in there. A friend of mine was sitting next to me Airmen Bill Macnamara and I told him what I had seen and he said he found a foot inside a military boot and he talked no more. No investigation or medic team came to us and ask anyone any questions if we saw and witnessed anything.

U.S.N. Airmen E-3 Paul Lester Cobble
#27 Mercedes Moreno St.
Aguadilla, PR 0063
07/11/15

8

Meeting at James J. Peters VA Medical Center Bronx, New York

John and Wes at James J. Peterson VA Medical Center Bronx New York

So, what if humanity doesn't care, no matter what you do to be triumphant, regardless of your circumstances? Eventually, over time, loneliness, unanswered questions, et cetera, shall wear you down to a point at which it becomes easy to become cognitively meek and week; thereby you eventually capitulate into believing that no one cares.

Then, too, after a while one becomes the victim to an energy and spirit that engulfs his or her social environment, making it extremely easier to assimilate and begin the process to not care. Like a subtle wave of wind energy that gusts and moves us as it passes, like stars that shoot through the open sky, it becomes just another seemingly thoughtless moment in time; it's so real but so unpredictable as time passes by.

These thoughts entered my head the morning after John and I met for the first time, after driving to meet with him at the James J. Peterson VA Medical Center located at 130 West Kingsbridge Road, Bronx, New York. It was on the evening of Tuesday, August 5, 2015.

It had been almost a year later, after I spoke with Tommy, and approximately a week or two removed from my thoughts about whether or not John was still alive after almost forty years removed from such a life-changing incident.

The following morning after our initial meeting, I took time to reflect upon and process the importance and value of the transaction between John and me. As my mind raced for the next answer to justify my trip to drive to the Bronx, New York, to meet, who I believe is a sterling example of the meaning of resiliency, strength and courage Mr. John Pugioti. I was also thankful, humble and understood that both of us were blessed to still be here on earth, at least in-part (I believe) because of the importance of sharing our story so that others shall benefit. That said, I knew that I would be remiss if there was no reflection from either John or me on how at least one of us felt during or after such an emotional moment. I believe that true reflection can have emotional value for someone in doubt or in need..

That said, security at the James J. Peters VA Medical Center Bronx New York was almost stifling, which, I can say begrudgingly, was a good thing because there is no doubt that it helps as a deterrent to the possibility of the threat of domestic and global terrorism. Being surrounded by federal police—they were everywhere, inside and outside of the building—I received a stark reminder of how the global society has stolen the innocence of our nation and the world's people in regards to how we interact with each other. Upon entering the federal building, I found it was similar to airport security, with X-ray technology machines and armed uniformed federal representatives with handheld metal detector wands, and they made everyone go through it, again, akin to an airport process or procedure for an individual to gain access to a federal airport or in this case a federal building.

That said, our meeting there was graciously allowed by a staff member whom I had contacted the day before. I shared with her our story and our plans to meet at the hospital, and how it would be beneficial to us if we could access a private area for John and me to meet for confidentiality purposes regarding other patients, staff members, et cetera. Thankfully, the volunteer services accommodated us with accesses to conference room 4D-53 on the fourth floor at 3:00 p.m. As I was waiting out in the parking lot for John to arrive in his vehicle at approximately 2:00 p.m., I exited my vehicle for a waiting area on hospital grounds to stretch my legs. While out there, somehow John parked and slipped pass me and entered the building to make his way up to our meeting room. He then sent me a text message stating he was up there in the conference room and asked me the question where was everybody at?

Minutes after his text, I was in the medical facility, exiting the elevator on the fourth floor, and soon as I turned the corner of the first hallway, I observed John sitting in his wheelchair down the hall, all alone in front of the conference room. As I observed and physically walked toward him, the reflection off of the shined highly buffed linoleum floors seemed to put a unique perspective on John and me meeting for the first time which was over thirty-seven years later after that dreadful evening on the flight deck of the USS *Forrestal CV-59*.

As I approached, a range of emotions overwhelmed me, some of which included sorrow and even a moral responsibility for the loss of John's limbs. Yes, I also felt somewhat awkward as I approached, and

I also for the first time in a long time I felt sort of speechless, partially because I fully expected him to be with some of his family members and others, but yet he sat there all alone.

The first words that came out of John's mouth were "Nobody cares." he went on to state that Tommy had a last-minute situation with his son that precluded him from coming, but he did not mention why his family members did not come, and I felt it was not my place to ask. In the moment, I briefly thought about it, thinking maybe it was because of my spontaneous arrival, meaning that I had said to John in late July that I would be driving to New York to meet him but had not given a specific date.

Then, on Monday, August 3, I called and shared with him that I would be leaving on Tuesday, heading to meet with him at the James J. Peterson VA Medical Center located at 130 West Kingsbridge Road, Bronx, New York.

Then, too, in the back of my mind, subconsciously, I still felt and herd something that said, "I have cost this man and his family enough grief, and now here I go opening up an old wound that they may have difficulty revisiting."

As I reflected upon it, John stated at least three to four times, immediately after entering the conference room, that "Nobody cares; it's been too long."

As I continued to reflect on the moment, I thought about the conversation we had earlier that morning at approximately 8:30 a.m. when I contacted John via text while I was in the office of volunteer services and inquired about what time he could be available to meet. On the phone, he did not seem overly excited; I think he did not believe that I would come, or he was in almost a form of shock to believe that I actually drove to speak with him. John then stated that he had his girlfriend over and wanted to spend time with her before he came. Moreover, he also stated that he had not seen her in a while and since his residence was in upstate New York approximately an hour from the James J. Peterson VA Medical Center that it would be at least until 3:00 p.m. before we could meet.

Somehow after getting there to meet, I felt that maybe John did not want to come himself. It was easy for me to drive to New York to visit and see him because I have both of my limbs. My traumatic experience that evening is absolutely nothing compared to the reality of John living a lifetime of trauma as a double amputee. Again, because of John's selflessness, I went to chow early that evening, and it was only because he chose to say, "You go eat first" that I did not become a double amputee or even killed during one of the most mishandled, highly probable cover-ups regarding an aircraft mishap on the flight deck of the USS *Forrestal CV-59*.

I can only imagine how agonizingly difficult it was for John to make the courageous decision to meet with me. I take my hat off to him and solute his bravery and perseverance as a strong-willed autonomous leader and a highly intelligent individual. Dressed in his silk Fourth of July summer shirt, John looked great, and as we sat in conference room 4B-53 from 3:00 p.m. till approximately 5:15 p.m., he articulated in a clear and concise manner how he felt about his life journey, the potential influence of our book, his family and friends, in addition to the past and continued challenges he faces as a double amputee. It was abundantly clear that he is easily a champion for veterans and other amputees who may be experiencing similar or greater challenges that could affect not only their quality of life but also their emotional and psychological well-being.

As we spoke and got even more comfortable with each other, John shared a story about how one of his closest friends and fellow motorcycle club member was riding his bike during a weekend of hard riding, and how it unfortunately resulted in him being a victim of a traumatic motorcycle accident.

Incredible as it may seem, his friend lost a limb in the incident as his bike careened out of control into a guard rail on a US interstate, resulting in him losing one of his legs. Ironically, after speaking and sharing information for over two hours during our initial meeting, the most stunning message shared with me by John was that of what he stated about how receptive his dear friend had become in regards to the reality of being an amputee. John stated, and I quote, "You are never are going to accept it; you're just going to learn to live with it." For me, his stated words are the most compelling words that I will ever remember from our first meeting in almost four decades, and I shall share and credit John with them for the remainder of my life, because to me those words are a look into his soul and virtue as a human being.

9

Manage Disappointment, Bureaucrats, Congressional Leaders

In my search for answers on the blistering cold Thursday of February 11, 2016, I attended an Armed Services Committee Meeting on the Future of Naval Aviation at the Rayburn House, located at 189 Russell Senate Office Building, Room # 2212, Washington DC while congress was in session. While I was there listening to the designated (by Congress) expert opinions of Dr. Cropsey, Dr. Horowitz, and CAPT., Robert C. "Barney" Rubel, USN Ret. Prof. Emeritus US Naval War College on the future viability of the US aircraft carrier and its carrier Air Wings, I had an opportunity to speak with some of the individuals who were guest attending the hearing itself just like I was.

I spoke with several people that day as I shared with them that I was there because I figured that maybe some individuals who were interested in naval aviation may also have some information that may lead me to the discovery of a pilot of a military aircraft that landed during re-spot on the flight deck of the USS *Forrestal CV-59* on the evening of January 15, 1978. It turned out that my hunch was somewhat correct; while I was speaking with CAPT., Rubel's wife, she stated that her husband, CAPT., Robert C. "Barney" Rubel, USN Ret., who was one of the three experts on the panel of speakers, had a chief petty officer (obviously this was while he was on active duty) who worked for him while they were stationed at NAS Cecile Field, Florida, and that the CPOs daughter use to babysit for them. She further stated to me without me saying anything other than I was primarily there attempting to find out some additional information about an aircraft mishap on the USS *Forrestal CV-59* on January 15, 1978 the following: "You mean the FID, and it was the XO of Attack Squadron VA-81," without me prompting her at all.

She further stated that she believed the name of the CPO who worked for her husband (CAPT., Rubel, USN Ret.) at that time was Johnson, but she was not exactly sure because it was so long ago. For me, I was astonished at what she said and understood that moment as being another piece of what we needed to help solve the puzzle, regardless of if the gentlemen (unidentified pilot) is still with us or not.

Our conversation took place while the committee meeting was in recess for approximately an hour because its congressional committee members had to go to the floor to cast a vote.

Prior to getting to room 2212, I visited the US Department of Veterans Affairs Office of Congressional & Legislative Affairs – Congressional Liaison Services and asked one of the congressional liaison representatives what would be the best course of action to finding out who the pilot was, and surprisingly, he shared some information that has the possibility of being very helpful. Unfortunately, that's a far cry from what I had been getting from the bureaucratic process, where you have to go through a plethora of gatekeepers, which, I believe, is a system designed to convince individuals to give up. Attempting to go through the traditional or established process of speaking with legislators on Capitol Hill is akin to drilling through a variety of levels of earth to just gain access to what you believe is what you have been searching for, only to discover that you spent a tremendous amount of time to get to the substance, but it's of no value to you.

With that said, I have discovered that as an advocate for veterans regarding legislative change, you have to go directly to the legislator's office in Washington, DC, regardless if he or she is in your district or not. From their perspective systemically, legislators have a number of effective methodologies and mechanisms that can frustrate, irritate, and cause you to capitulate, in regards to bringing a situation that is important to you to their attention. Therefore, one must take a non-traditional approach to gain their attention and not become satisfied with a conversation either on the phone or in person with a junior fellow, who basically is just an errand or messenger person and whom the legislator doesn't even know exists half the time (depending on the legislator), because they are so caught up in the politics of the moment, as they are dedicated to satisfying the individuals who have or are currently financing their campaigns.

Some bureaucratic tactics that you may encounter include:

1. I only meet constituents who have issues dealing with veterans in my hometown district.

2. I only speak with individuals in my district.

3. I am busy; you have to get an appointment.

4. You have to go to my official website and send me an email, and I will get back with you on that.

5. Talk to my fellow; he or she will get the information to me, and I will have someone contact you.

6. The congressmen will contact you when Congress is back in session.

Far too often you never speak with the legislator you are seeking, and if you finally get a response, it's usually based upon a predetermined priority matrix based upon a bureaucracy of young fellows who initially may get excited in their eagerness to assist you after they hear your initial request, but almost immediately after they speak with their supervisor, if it's something they don't really value, then the excitement exhibited just moments earlier may become tapered. Hence, it is to your advantage to take your case to the legislators themselves; as you walk the halls of Congress many times, by default you will have opportunities for moments of spontaneous engagement as you will routinely see some of your most influential legislators walking the halls. Frequently, they are unaccompanied, without their designated gatekeepers, and when the opportunity arises, be ready to engage them in a friendly, logical, intellectual conversation, but ensure that you end it by giving him or her your business card. Actually, in person, many of them are nice people and will talk with you. But remain cognizant of the fact that, if your issue is something that can benefit their agenda, then you have a great shot of capturing their ear. However, make sure that your elevator pitch is of the fine-tuned brand; that is sweet music to their ears.

Epilogue

As the "Leading Authority on Military Veterans and Anger Management," I have assisted a plethora (too many to number) of veterans and civilians whose anger has been rooted in past experiences, some of which have been traumatizing and are at the root of characteristics associated with PTSD and some have been a result of assimilating to the toxicity within their environment, while some exhibit a combination of each of what was stated.

Wes speaking to Homeless Veterans Homeless Stand Down in Tampa, Florida

From my experience many maladaptive-behaving individuals I have assisted, have never questioned their behavior, and if they have, it's only when they have crossed over the line and require intervention motivated by their need to adhere to law enforcement requests, court orders, or the fulfillment of some other kind of mandate. In fact, it's a rarity when adults (especially business executives) initiate actions to gain what I believe are invaluable soft skills training to address possible deficiencies in regards to leadership and basic communication skills, especially when they have unchallenged authority with zero accountability for their maladaptive behavior.

Mark Jagger, unidentified veteran, Wes, at Homeless Stand Down, Tampa, Florida

That said, the success of building strong and cohesive human relationships begins with the fundamental skills of interpersonal and intrapersonal communication skills—they are inseparable. The relationship between John and me was severed on January 15, 1978. For over thirty-seven years I have (and I have no doubt that other shipmates have thought about him also) thought about what happened to the young Italian man from New York who lost his legs that evening on the flight deck of my first ship, the USS *Forrestal* CV-59.

Moreover, in both the past and even more so now that we have been communicating with each other for the past year and a half, I have wondered, and I am sure John has too, what would my life look like today if, instead of John being the one who lost his legs, I had lost mine? It took me going to a three-day Veterans Homeless Stand Down in Tampa, Florida, in 2015 to understand the impact of the magnitude and concept of moral injury trauma. To never forget John's last name and often visualizing his name in the Blue shirt locker stenciled with red spray paint in big bold letters, with running lines of red (from overspray), which again appeared to me and others' who also observed it that evening because we discussed it as being an eerie sign to avoid writing one's name in red. It left an indelible image in my mind and ultimately a sense of responsibility that has never gone away, but fate has a way of connecting or filling the dots.

Therefore (from my perspective) individuals who are cognizant of the value of a balanced approach to life can better accept fate in the mist of time regardless if situations or actions do not play out or are perceived to be in their favor at a particular moment in time. As a proponent and advocate of the concept and theories associated with gestalt, I most strongly believe that it all balances out for what it's worth at some point in time. With that said, artificial intelligence may not be authentic from a communication standpoint and perspective, but it's the game changer that answered both John's and my individual burning desire to discover each other and to reconnect for the purpose of answering our unanswered questions about the evening of January 15, 1978.

Just think about it , on May 23, 2014, I posted an article on LinkedIn Pulse, a writer's forum of LinkedIn.com, entitled: "Let's 'Never Forget' the Sailors of the USS Forrestal CV-59" as a tribute to our fallen and injured shipmates, on Memorial Day 2014. It was my way of showing the world that I have not forgotten what happened that evening and showing gratitude for being blessed to have both of my legs and how it not only changed my perspective on life but changed the social and family dynamics for countless others whom I have met and never met.

On Friday evening September 12, 2014, I received an unknown phone call with an out of state zip code and number that I had no familiarity with; typically I don't answer unknown calls because too many times they are annoying salespeople, solicitors, or worse than that, nemeses from the past (relatives included) perpetrating as if they have your best interest when all they really and only want is information from you to determine if you are as miserable as they are during the time of their contact.

However, for some reason, I was cognizant that a few days earlier I had a premonition that caused me to wonder if Pugiotl was still alive; in fact, in the original article on LinkedIn, I called him Dave Pajettie. I misspelled his last name and completely whiffed on his first name, in part because while in the military we more times than not would call each other by our last names, basically ignoring our first names and as for Johns last name, I misspelled it because it's Italian, and candidly speaking, I knew no Italians prior to military service. It was an honest mistake on my part, however to me one of the more important things that mattered was that others would get an opportunity to learn about our story; it was the other promise that I had made to myself on that awful evening, which was to take advantage of life's second chance.

As God would have it, John, being the loyal and fierce competitor that he is, had not given up and had been searching for more than thirty-six years for someone who could shed some light on what happened that evening. Moreover, he had a New York City firefighter friend who took it upon himself to do some research on the internet for John, and he was the one on the other end of the line of that unknown phone call with the out of state zip code and number. I found out because I checked my only phone message and a voice stated something to the effect of "Were you on the USS *Forrestal* in 1978 and worked on the flight deck with John Pugioti?" In somewhat of a shock as I remember beginning to breath hard, I hurriedly called the number he left and after I Identified myself, I responded to his question with something like "Pugioti got his legs cut off. Yes, I served with him in V-1 Division."

Shortly after and still stunned (I believe both of us were) because of the magnitude of what both of us had just heard, I was informed that John was still alive and that he had no knowledge of what really trans-pired on the evening of January 15, 1978, and he was desperately seeking information and answers about the aircraft mishap and the entire situation. In a fog, somehow I believe he told me to standby and that he would call me back after he spoke with John because it would be very emotional for him to talk with me because he had not spoken to any of his shipmates who did not get injured during his "final re-spot" on that tragic evening.

As a result of his friend's research and approximately ten to twenty minutes later I received a call from my old shipmate; we had not spo-ken with or seen each other for more than thirty-six years. An emo-tional reunion via the medium of technology had been initiated. As John wept, I attempted to suppress my excitement at being reunited with the man who volunteered to stay on the flight deck of the FID in Fly-3 (not knowing that it would become an infamous evening) and allow me to go to chow first, which in essence led to a tale of two young sailors, one African American and the other an Italian American, who shall forever be bonded together because of one tragic incident in US Naval Aviation history. Consequently, after that evening, each of our lives evolved into two very different stories re-garding the maturation process and the quality of our individual lives.

As I shared with John what happened that evening, he expressed his feelings of relief that he had finally validated in part at least a piece of his military service and the reason he was so unfortunate to have lost his legs that evening during an event that the Navy has kept silent about or minimized for almost four decades.

Shortly after the initial contact, John and I spoke again via phone and shared sea stories about shipmates, ports of call, family, friends, and the path of our careers, challenges, and so forth. Later, after several contacts, I asked John if he would agree to collaborate with me on writing and sharing our story, utilizing the very technology that facilitated our being connected together for the writing of this book. Obviously he agreed, but he also stated that he had made numerous contacts with various celebrity morning show hosts soliciting their assistance in helping him find out what happened to him on the evening of January 15, 1978, but never received interest from anyone.

So, for me, and from my experience as the "Leading Authority on Military Veterans and Anger Management" and being the Principal Consultant of GCS Facilitators and Consultants, it is easy to see how the secondary emotion of anger has perpetually been a challenge for John for the almost forty years since the mishap on the evening of January 15, 1978.

One of the things John shared with me initially, after I shared with him what profession I transitioned into after retirement from the United States Navy in September of 1996, was that I would not be able to fix his anger. When he stated that to me, I smiled because I totally and wholeheartedly agreed with John and his opinion on his challenge with anger, and here are some reasons why I smiled.

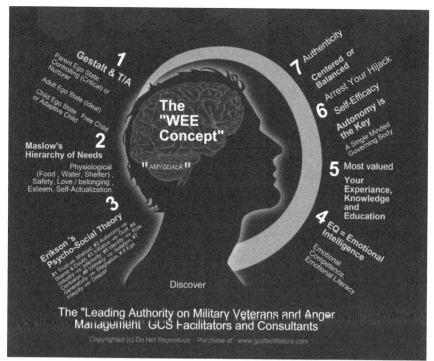

1 Gestalt & T/A
Parent Ego State: Controlling (Critical) or Nurturer
Adult Ego State (Ideal)
Child Ego State: Free Child or Adaptive Child

The "WEE Concept"

2 Maslow's Hierarchy of Needs
Physiological (Food , Water, Shelter) , Safety, Love / belonging , Esteem, Self-Actualization.

3 Erikson's Psycho-Social Theory
#1 Trust- vs - Mistrust, #2 Autonomy -vs - #4 Industry - vs - Inferiority, #6 Intimacy -vs - Isolation, #7 Generativity -vs - Stagnation, # 8 Ego Integrity -vs- Despair. Shame & Doubt, #3 Initiative -vs- Guilt, #4 Role Confusion, #5 Identity -vs-

AMYGDALA

Discover

7 Authenticity
Centered or Balanced
Arrest Your Hijack

6 Self-Efficacy
Autonomy is the Key
A Single Minded Governing Body

5 Most valued
Your Experiance, Knowledge and Education

4 EQ = Emotional Intelligence
Emotional Competence.
Emotional Literacy

The "Leading Authority on Military Veterans and Anger Management GCS Facilitators and Consultants

The "WEE Concept" an award-winning curriculum developed by Wesley E. Etheridge Sr.

First and foremost, as a Grand Canyon State Diplomate Certified Anger Management Facilitator /Coach (DCAMF) and behavioral influencer who is adept at utilizing our award-winning eclectic curriculum and approach for behavioral modification, (affectionately known as the "WEE Concept") I am passionate and adamant about sharing with others that the value in our methodology is the fact that "we don't fix anyone's anger. We simply "assist them with discovering themselves."

Second, as a colleague and shipmate of John's, I feel somewhat in-debted to him for my entire military career, post-military career, and the quality of my social life. So, I would not be the one to challenge John with challenging his fear of managing his anger when I very well understand that he has unanswered questions from his military experience that has hindered him from embracing his secondary emotion of anger as just a component of his primary ego state.

Third, more than anything I share with all who will listen, that changing one's situational dynamics can be initiated by an autonomous individual who is cognizant of the opportunities that are ahead of them and at this time in John's life, I intuitively feel that my brother John Pugioti is trending in the right direction. Thank you for taking a fragment of your precious time to read this valued story. With that said, if your organization is seeking speakers for your program, school, or agency, please consider requesting John and me as we travel on our nationwide author and book-signing tour and while we share at veterans service organizations, VA medical facilities, veterans homeless shelters, Veterans Stand Downs, and other places that value stories about resilience, strength, and the human spirit as we embrace opportunities to inform the nation about a tragedy and a wonderful human interest story of a young sailor's triumph over the most arduous and adverse conditions, which were exacerbated by not knowing for more than three decades what actually transpired on the evening of January 15, 1978. Within itself, this book in part is one of the numerous components that is being utilized in regards to our proactive approach (in what is arguably society's most advanced technological age) to continue to gather evidence and solicit new information that could potentially assist both John and me in discovering more answers in regards to the reason why January 15, 1978, became a quality-of-life challenge for all involved and a central game-changing event for our lifetimes and the subject for the writing of "My Final Re-spot."

If you enjoyed some of the philosophies within this book, please review my Supplemental Behavioral Influencer Guide entitled "Manage Your Anger In Ten Days" on Amazon.com and connect with both John and me on LinkedIn.com, either prior to or after you initiate a review regarding your thoughts about our book on all social media platforms, because your review could be the single reason that some veteran or someone else does not make an attempt to hurt themselves our others because he or she is struggling with chronic or acute anger. Also, if you happen to be in the Washington, DC, metro area, and you would like to request John and I to speak at your corporate event or for your group of transitioning veterans, et cetera, please visit the GCS Facilitators and Consultants website at: www.gcsfacilitators.com and enter your request for an appointment in the request information form at the top of the landing page, or call and make an appointment at (202) 867- 8344 to visit us at the GCS Facilitators and Consultants Corporate Office, located at: 1025 Connecticut Ave., NW., STE 1000, Washington, DC 20036. DCAMF.

CPSIA information can be obtained
at www.ICGtesting.com
Printed in the USA
BVHW041225181221
624353BV00001B/65